THE CERAMIC ART
OF KOREA

PLATE I. See page 222

THE
CERAMIC ART
OF
KOREA

edited by
DR. CHEWON KIM
Director of the National Museum of Korea
and
G. ST. G. M. GOMPERTZ

FABER AND FABER LIMITED
24 Russell Square
London

First published in mcmlxi
by Faber and Faber Limited
24 Russell Square, London, W.C.1
Printed in Great Britain
by R. MacLehose and Company Limited
All rights reserved

PLATES

[7]

PLATES

YI DYNASTY
(A.D. 1392–1910)

PLATES

INTRODUCTION

A BRIEF HISTORY OF KOREAN CERAMIC ART

The prehistoric pottery of Korea is a plain coarse ware, reddish brown in colour, the predominant shape being that of a pot with a straight neck and flat base. In addition, there are two varieties which show outside influence, the first being pottery with comb patterns (*kamm keramik*) and the second polished reddish pottery. The first of these is probably related to the Scandinavian comb-pattern pottery and the second to the painted pottery of China, which has a range extending to South Manchuria. About the end of the prehistoric era a fresh wave of foreign influence, mainly from China, becomes evident: a new type of grey stoneware resulted and later developed into the Silla period pottery, which was made in such abundance in South Korea.

In the north the kingdom of Koguryŏ (*c.* 37 B.C.–A.D. 668) came under direct Chinese influence, both from the Chinese colony of Lo-lang established in northern Korea and from China itself. Two kinds of pottery were produced — plain grey and glazed. Very little has survived, however, so that our knowledge of Koguryŏ pottery is scanty, but it seems clear that the ware is akin to Han pottery and much softer than the grey pottery of South Korea.

The pottery of the kingdom of Paekche (*c.* 18 B.C.–A.D. 663) in south-western Korea also came under the influence of the Chinese pottery of Lo-lang. It has been divided into three groups — grey or brownish earthenware, glazed earthenware and grey stoneware. The first kind resembles Lo-lang pottery in appearance and quality; it is frequently ornamented with the so-called mat pattern. The second kind may also be related to Lo-lang pottery, but some of the vessels exhibit influence from South China. The third group is similar in quality to Silla pottery, but the shapes of the vessels are different.

POTTERY WARES OF THE SILLA PERIOD
(*c.* 57 B.C.–A.D. 935)

'Silla pottery' is the term commonly applied to the grey stoneware which was made so abundantly in South Korea during the Silla period. It was derived from the plain brownish pottery of prehistoric Korea under the influence of China and shows an affinity with the greyish pottery of the pre-Han and Han eras. The hardness of Silla pottery, however, cannot be found in other contemporary Far Eastern pottery and must be regarded as a distinctive achievement of the potters of southern Korea. In the fourth century A.D. Silla pottery completed a development which had been taking place from the first century. The history of Silla pottery is divisible into two main periods, as follows:

(a) FIRST PERIOD

This period lasted approximately two centuries, from the late fourth century A.D. to the end of the sixth century. During this time the kingdom of Silla was one of the three kingdoms of Korea, the other two being Paekche and Koguryŏ. Numerous tumuli of great size were constructed in this period. All contained large quantities of Silla pottery. In some cases a separate chamber was provided for storage of the funerary gifts, which consisted mainly of pottery. Sometimes over three hundred pottery vessels were found in a single chamber.

Silla pottery of this period is grey in colour, varying from a light to a dark tone. The clay was carefully selected, but sometimes it contains small pieces of quartz. The pottery was fired at a relatively high temperature, resulting in porcellanous hardness. No glaze was applied at this date; however, very frequently the so-called 'natural glaze' (i.e. kiln gloss) may be observed, derived from the silicon content of the clay. Predominant vessel types are the covered cup on a tall, openwork foot (Plate 4) and the jar with a cylindrical neck, sometimes having an openwork foot and sometimes not (Plate 2). The covered cup has a characteristic knob on top of the cover and one or two rows of rectangular openings in the foot, but occasionally triangular or circular openings are found. These Silla cups were used as food containers, like the Chinese *tou*. Often they have been excavated with shells or other remains of foodstuffs inside. A prototype is found in prehistoric Korean pottery, and some connection may be traced with the similar pottery *tou* recovered in South Manchuria. The jar has a tall cylindrical neck, a round body and rounded base. Some examples have a short foot but others have none. The former were used as food containers, while the latter may have served as water carriers. There are also many other shapes among the Silla pottery wares, such as drinking cups, cups without any foot, pottery stands, etc.

Most of the Silla pottery made in the first period was decorated with incised geometrical patterns, such as wavy lines, triangles, circles, zig-zags, vertical parallel lines, dotted lines, etc. During the fifth and sixth centuries Silla pottery reached its zenith: typical examples have been recovered from the Gold Crown Tomb and Gold Bell Tomb, both at Kyŏngju.

Besides these ordinary or utilitarian vessels there are clay figurines and fanciful shapes. The mounted figure excavated in 1924 from the Gold Bell Tomb at Kyŏngju (Plate 3) is an outstanding example of the clay figurines, remarkable for its naïve and naturalistic treatment and entirely dissimilar to Chinese clay figurines.

[12]

POTTERY WARES OF THE SILLA PERIOD

(b) SECOND PERIOD

The three centuries from the seventh to the early tenth century comprise the second period of Silla pottery. During the latter half of the seventh century Silla unified the whole peninsula by overthrowing the kingdoms of Paekche and Koguryŏ. For this reason the kingdom of Silla before the unification is known as 'Old Silla', and afterwards it is called 'Unified Silla' or 'Great Silla'.

During this second period the people of Silla discontinued the construction of large tombs; instead, they cremated the bodies of the dead, as enjoined by Buddhist doctrine, and placed the ashes in urns. The Silla pottery of this period accordingly consists mainly of these burial urns. The shapes include ovoid jars with covers, cylindrical boxes with covers, long-necked bottles, covered bowls, cups on feet, etc. With the exception of the last-named type, all these are new forms created in this period. The cups on feet are dissimilar to those of the first period, having short, clumsy feet with a few very small holes, often almost invisible and sometimes entirely absent. Jars with long necks are no longer found. As shown in Plate 5, the burial urns were usually covered with floral and geometrical decoration. A significant change from the first period is that both the designs and the method of decoration are different. Instead of being incised as in the first period, the designs were stamped. Furthermore, yellowish brown or olive glazes appear for the first time on these urns, resulting — it is supposed — from contact with the ceramic art of Paekche and Koguryŏ.

After a while Silla pottery began to degenerate. It became a less prominent part of the popular culture, either because the people lost interest in wares executed in monochrome or because they employed more vessels made from other materials, such as wood, lacquer and metal. However, the grey stoneware survived as a lower class of pottery during the Koryŏ period (A.D. 918–1392): it was used by the common people, probably for the storage of food, whereas the famed Koryŏ celadons became the vessels in which food was served.

POTTERY WARES OF THE KORYŎ PERIOD
(A.D. 918–1392)

Both in China and Korea the five centuries from the beginning of the tenth century to the end of the fourteenth constituted the golden age of ceramic art. In China during this period fine celadons and white porcelains were produced at such famous potteries as Yüeh-chou, Ting-chou, Tz'u-chou and Ching-tê Chên. At first the ceramic art of the Koryŏ period was influenced by that of Sung China, combining a classical style with remarkable proficiency in technique. The elegant forms, rich colour and unique inlaid technique of Koryŏ pottery stand out as a major achievement in this field.

The development of Koryŏ pottery may be divided into four periods, as follows:

[13]

POTTERY WARES OF THE KORYŎ PERIOD

(a) TRANSITIONAL PERIOD

This period roughly comprised the tenth century, during which the traditional grey Silla ware continued to be predominant; however, by the end of the century the prototype of celadon ware had made its appearance.

(b) PERIOD OF CHINESE INFLUENCE

From about the end of the tenth century Koryŏ pottery began to reflect the influence of Chinese celadon, both in the forms of vessels and their technique.

(c) PERIOD OF KORYŎ CELADON WARE

By the twelfth century Koryŏ ceramic art had become independent of Chinese influence and had developed a native Koryŏ celadon ware with its own distinctive style, colour and technique. The colour, which was known as 'Koryŏ pi-saek' (strictly 'Koryŏ kingfisher colour'), and the graceful forms are typically Korean.

(d) PERIOD OF DECLINE

By the end of the thirteenth century a fresh wave of influence from Yüan China had reached Korea. This found expression in novel designs and methods of decoration, but it undermined the native Koryŏ tradition. With the decadence of the nation, the brilliant achievement of Koryŏ celadon ware had become a thing of the past by the end of the fourteenth century.

Most of the Koryŏ pottery which has survived was found in tombs. The Japanese were captivated by the beauty of Koryŏ celadon, with the result that hitherto undisturbed tombs around Kaesŏng and elsewhere were pillaged from the beginning of the present century. Many specimens of Koryŏ celadon also went overseas, and their unique qualities attracted connoisseurs as well as scholars in all parts of the world.

The pottery of the Koryŏ period may be classified as follows:

(1) PLAIN CELADON

This is the celadon ware produced before the development of the *sanggam*, or inlaid, technique. The early Koryŏ celadons reflected the style and technique of Chinese Yüeh ware of the Five Dynasties and Sung periods. However, Koryŏ celadon soon became distinguished for its fine, bluish green glaze, which was called *pi-saek* as stated above. *Pi-saek* celadon ware flourished during the eleventh and twelfth centuries, and it was during this hundred-and-fifty odd years that most of the graceful vessels with incised or relief decoration were produced.

(2) INLAID (*Sanggam*) CELADON

The technique of inlaying porcelain was invented by the Korean potters. It is a method of decoration in which the pattern was first incised and then filled with white or black slip. Any excess slip was smoothed away and the vessel was fired. After this it was covered with a celadon glaze (i.e. a glaze containing iron) and refired. According to some authorities, however, only a single firing took place and there was no preliminary low-temperature or biscuit firing. Sometimes iron or copper oxides were used for additional decoration: the copper produced a reddish colour after the firing, while the iron produced a rust colour. The technique of inlaying was probably developed about the middle of the twelfth century — as will be discussed in detail below.

(3) PAINTED CELADON

This type of celadon was painted with white slip, black slip or iron oxide under the glaze. The majority of specimens decorated in this way exhibit the influence of the northern Chinese Tz'u-chou potteries of the Yüan or early Ming period. This technique continued to the end of the Koryŏ dynasty.

(4) WHITE PORCELAIN

Koryŏ white porcelain is called '*paek-Koryŏ*' ('white Koryŏ') in Korean. The technique was known from an early date as a result of the importation of Sung white wares. Koryŏ white porcelain exhibits either the bluish tone of Chinese *ying-ch'ing* ware or the ivory colour of Ting ware. Incised or impressed decoration was the rule, but sometimes openwork designs or inlaying were employed (Plate 61). Scholars had long questioned whether any of the white porcelains found in Korea were actually made there, but all doubts were dispelled by the discovery of a kiln-site with numerous white shards dating from the Koryŏ period at Yuch'ŏn-ri, Puan-gun, Chŏlla Puk-do, in the south-western part of the peninsula.

(5) IRON-BLACK WARE

This ware was made of the same greyish clay as that used for ordinary Koryŏ celadon. However, it was first coated with an iron pigment before application of the glaze. Some pieces are plain, without decoration, but others have incised patterns through the iron pigment, with the result that the grey colour of the body stands out against the dark background and often assumes a green tone owing to the glaze being of celadon type.

[15]

There are also specimens on which designs were painted with white slip over the iron pigment. It is believed that this type of iron-black ware was produced for only a few decades from the end of the twelfth century to the early thirteenth.

(6) IRON-GLAZED WARE

The red-brown colour of this pottery is caused by the high percentage of iron in the glaze. Usually the surface was left plain, without decoration; however, there are some examples with patterns made by scraping away the background and filling this with white slip.

(7) UNGLAZED POTTERY

This is either light or dark pottery ware without glaze. Some pieces were fired at a high temperature, others at a low. They were probably used as kitchen wares by the common people of Koryŏ.

(8) BLACK-GLAZED WARE

This is the pottery with a thick glaze of black or dark brown colour, known by the Japanese name *temmoku*. A considerable number of these wares were made in the late Koryŏ period and have survived to this day.

(9) MISCELLANEOUS WARES

The olive or brownish glaze characteristic of the early Koryŏ period continued in use to the end of the dynasty. Pottery with glazes of various other colours also were made during the late Koryŏ period. A few examples are known where inlaid celadons were gilded, that is to say the designs were outlined in gold over the glaze. There are also specimens which have designs painted in thick white slip, so that the decoration appears embossed under the glaze. Other types of ware were sprayed with iron glaze or coated with a layer of lacquer; and a few specimens of marbled ware have been found. However, celadon was without question the main product throughout the period. The study of Koryŏ celadon and investigation of kiln-sites has not yet been completed, and the early stages of development in particular are still obscure.

The jar shown in Plate 6 probably represents the earliest type of glazed Koryŏ pottery. The inscription on its base reads: 'Made in the fourth year of Soon-hwa (the Sung era *Shun-hua*) . . . for use in the First Room of the Shrine of King T'aejo, by the potter Choi Kil-hwoi.' The jar has a porcellanous body, and the glaze shows some crazing and is similar to that of Yüeh celadon ware of the Five Dynasties period (907–960). It is accordingly believed that the prototype of celadon ware originated late in the tenth century.

About the middle of the eleventh century the Koryŏ potters are thought to have

[16]

succeeded in making true celadon ware. The earliest record of Koryǒ celadon is found in the Chinese work *Hsüan-ho Fêng-shih Kao-li T'u-ching*, or 'Illustrated Account of the Envoy to Koryǒ in the Hsüan-ho Era' by Hsü Ching, who came to Kaesǒng with the Sung envoy in the year 1123. The record has survived but without the illustrations and states: 'Many vessels are of gold or silver, but the green pottery ware is outstanding' (Chapter 26). Hsü Ching also remarks: 'The pottery is green in colour and is called "*pi-saek*" by the Koreans; of late the workmanship has greatly improved and the colour and glaze are unsurpassed' (Chapter 32).

Hsü Ching's valuable record shows that a considerable amount of celadon ware with a fine bluish green glaze had been produced by the early part of the twelfth century, some being in the Chinese style but some distinctively Korean. It is difficult to give a precise date for the origin of Koryǒ celadon ware, but there are good grounds for believing that it was first produced about the middle of the eleventh century. The arguments for this may be summarized as follows:

(1) During the reign of King Munjong (1047–83) the civil and military organization of the Koryǒ State had become firmly established, with the result that circumstances were favourable for cultural developments.

(2) It was also in King Munjong's reign that cultural relations with Sung China were fostered.

(3) During the early Sung period, from the late tenth century to the middle of the eleventh, the technique of making celadon ware was perfected in China and the potteries were expanded and went into mass production.

(4) It was probably at this time, i.e. the mid-eleventh century, that the celadon technique of Chekiang, as represented by Yüeh ware, reached the Puan and Kangjin districts in the southern coastal region of Korea and gave fresh stimulus to the Korean celadon kilns.

During the latter half of the eleventh century Koryǒ celadon must have made rapid progress. In addition to the record of Hsü Ching we have the evidence of several specimens of plain celadon excavated from the tomb of King Injong (reigned 1123–46), among which was the lobed vase illustrated in Plate 22. By the early part of the twelfth century the beautiful 'kingfisher colour' had been developed and the forms had acquired a typically Korean gracefulness. The potters produced celadons with incised or impressed decoration and vessels in human or animal form which demonstrate their inventive skill. However, it seems that they were more concerned to perfect the colour of the glaze than to produce original shapes and designs. The colour of Koryǒ celadon ware was regarded by contemporary Chinese as one of the world's outstanding achievements.

The plain celadons with 'kingfisher coloured' glaze were followed by the unique inlaid celadons. The earliest datable examples of inlaid celadon known are a small dish with inlaid chrysanthemum design and a bowl inlaid with floral arabesques (Plate 32), both of which were found in a stone coffin with an epitaph dated the thirteenth year of

[17]

King Ŭijong, corresponding to 1159. Another early example is a bowl with inlaid pomegranate decoration which was found, together with three inlaid dishes, in the tomb of King Myŏngjong (reigned 1170–97).

Since the technique of inlaying is not mentioned in Hsü Ching's record of 1123 but had reached a very advanced stage by the reign of King Myŏngjong, or towards the end of the century, we may suppose that it was invented in the early part of King Injong's reign (1123–46) soon after Hsü Ching's visit. Inlaid celadon ware came into full flower during the latter half of the twelfth century, and painted designs as well were also sometimes employed.

At the beginning of the thirteenth century a new development took place. Up to this time the Koryŏ potters had fired their celadons in a reducing atmosphere, which was effective in producing the pure bluish green colour; but now they began to use an oxidizing atmosphere, resulting in brown or yellowish tones. No doubt this was largely because they were no longer proficient at the difficult technique by which they obtained the earlier, blue-toned celadons, and there are many examples of wares partly suffused with brown as a result of 'mis-firing'. Koryŏ celadon ware now began to decline, and the country was ravaged by the Mongol invasion from 1231 onwards. Although some Yüan influence is apparent in the vessels produced from about this time, inlaid celadon continued to be the main product throughout the thirteenth century.

The *Koryŏ-sa*, or History of the Koryŏ Dynasty, describes the presentation of inlaid celadons from Koryŏ to the Yüan Court. The designs on some of the vessels were embellished with overglaze gilding. One example of this type was found at the palace-site in Kaesŏng and still shows traces of the gold (Plate 50). However, the glaze itself is no longer the famous 'kingfisher colour' of earlier times.

Koryŏ celadon degenerated steadily during the latter part of the thirteenth century, and in the fourteenth the fine inlaying technique was replaced by the easier method of stamping a design, resulting in overall decoration of stylized floral patterns. The clay was no longer carefully selected and the colour of the glaze had become impure.

The Koryŏ kiln-sites are widely scattered from the Kangsŏ district in the north of Korea to that of Kangjin in the extreme south-west. However, the main centres were in the south around Puan and Kangjin. Surviving examples of Koryŏ pottery have mostly come from the region of Kaesŏng, the former capital. Many also have come from the island of Kanghwa, not far from Seoul, where the capital was established for nearly forty years during the Mongol occupation.

POTTERY WARES OF THE YI PERIOD
(A.D. 1392–1910)

There are two basic types of pottery among the Yi period wares: the first is called *punch'ŏng* ware and is actually a transformation of Koryŏ celadon, while the second is white porcelain and was also derived from the white porcelain of the Koryŏ period. Generally speaking, the pottery wares of the Yi period lack the delicate craftsmanship observed in Koryŏ pottery. The forms are simple and robust, the colours and styles direct and unsophisticated. If Koryŏ pottery is considered aristocratic, Yi pottery must be regarded as plebeian. This characteristic reflects the pattern of Yi period culture in general.

The history of Yi pottery may be divided into two periods, with the Japanese invasion of 1592–8 as the dividing-line. During the Japanese invasion the ceramic industry of Korea sustained serious damage: numerous potteries were destroyed and the potters themselves seized and carried off to Japan. The technique of making white porcelain managed to survive, but *punch'ŏng* ware failed to reappear after the invasion.

During the first period, which roughly covers the two centuries from the late fourteenth to the end of the sixteenth, there was steady development in Yi ceramic art. *Punch'ŏng* ware, following in the tradition of Koryŏ celadon — though having a widely different character from its prototype — was produced in large quantity during this period; likewise white porcelain, plain or with underglaze blue decoration, progressed steadily. The latter shows strong influence from Ming blue-and-white. It is recorded that there were two hundred and twenty-one official or government-operated kilns, apart from privately operated kilns, during the reign of King Sejong (1419–50).

However, the Japanese invasion interrupted the development of Yi ceramic art, and the production of *punch'ŏng* ware was obliterated. Kilns making other types suffered heavy losses, and the Yi Court had difficulty in finding kilns to furnish vessels for their own use. The Japanese invaders not only destroyed the pottery kilns but carried off many of the potters to Japan. Korean pottery had become treasured by the Japanese as vessels for use in the Tea Ceremony, and the motive in seizing the Korean potters was to have these valued tea-bowls made directly in Japan. Accordingly, the Korean potters taken to Japan were placed under the protection of the Daimyōs and laid the foundations of the famed Japanese porcelain industry.

After the Japanese invasion white porcelain decorated with underglaze blue became the main product of the Yi potteries. Various other types, such as porcelain with underglaze iron-brown and copper-red decoration, also were produced. The Punwŏn kiln centre near Kwangju, east of Seoul, was operated by the Government and remained the most active pottery throughout the seventeenth, eighteenth and nineteenth centuries, the major product being blue-and-white. In 1883 the Punwŏn kilns were turned over to a private company as a result of the financial straits of the Government. By that time Japanese political influence was already permeating the country, and the company employed Japanese potters in order to modernize the project. This brought about a confusion of different ceramic techniques and hastened the decline of the Yi pottery tradition. The final closure of the Punwŏn kilns marks the end of Yi period blue-and-white.

We give below a brief description of the main types of ware made in the Yi period:

[19]

POTTERY WARES OF THE YI PERIOD

(1) PUNCH'ŎNG WARE

Punch'ŏng ware is made of the same greyish clay as Koryŏ celadon, though it is somewhat coarser in texture. The surface is covered either partially or completely with a brushed coating of white slip. Sometimes, instead of using a brush, the potters placed the vessels in a large tray filled with white slip. The vessels coated with brushed slip show traces of the swift strokes of a broad brush. It is this kind of brush mark that exhibits the carefree, artless character of Yi pottery in the highest degree. There are also specimens without an over-all coating of white slip: instead, tiny floral patterns or simple dots were stamped into the surface, and these stamped patterns were filled with brushed white slip after the general style of inlaid celadon ware of the Koryŏ period. Sometimes a bold design was freely incised in the body and carefully filled with white or black slip, a technique identical to that of inlaying Koryŏ celadon. In addition, there are examples in which the stamping and inlaying methods were used together.

Besides the above, there are also some other variations, such as designs incised in a white body or made by scraping away the white background in sgraffiato style so that the pattern stands out by itself, and designs painted in underglaze iron on a white body.

Punch'ŏng ware in general is a transformation of Koryŏ celadon. The application of white slip and overall decorative patterns were employed to distract the eye from the poor, greyish blue tone of the body and glaze; however, it must be admitted that the pottery is novel in type and entirely characteristic of the Yi period. The exact date when *punch'ŏng* ware first appeared is uncertain, but it was being produced in fully developed form in southern Korea at the beginning of the fifteenth century, and it continued to be made until the end of the sixteenth century.

Further particulars of *punch'ŏng* ware and the exact meaning of the term are given in the description of Plate 71.

(2) PLAIN WHITE PORCELAIN

Yi white porcelain of the first period, though derived from the white porcelain of the Koryŏ period, is characterized by a robust form, thick potting and the solid texture of the white colour. We no longer see the *ying-ch'ing* bluish tone or ivory tone of the Koryŏ white wares. During the second period, however, the tone again became slightly bluish white and has been likened to that of clear water. Masterpieces for the writer's desk — brush stands, water pots, water droppers, etc. — were produced in the second period. The plain white pots of tall ovoid shape and creamy white texture belong to the latter part of this period. White porcelains were produced all over the country, but the finest pieces come from the Punwŏn kilns near Seoul.

(3) BLUE-AND-WHITE PORCELAIN

It seems likely that the technique of early Ming blue-and-white reached Korea in the

[20]

late Koryŏ or early Yi period. By the beginning of the fifteenth century white porcelain with underglaze blue decoration was being produced in Korea with the use of imported cobalt. In 1464 local government officials discovered cobalt ore in Korea, and the designs were painted with this indigenous material.

Probably one of the earliest datable specimens of Yi blue-and-white porcelain is a bowl in the collection of Mr Hyung-pil Chun of Seoul (Plate 87). This bowl is inscribed in underglaze blue on the base with the characters 'Chung Shik' and is believed to have been specially made for a person of this name who passed the national examination in 1432 and later became a high-ranking official in the Government. The bowl is thought to have been made in the latter half of the fifteenth century, and the dark, impure colour of the blue suggests that the domestic cobalt may have been used.

Blue-and-white porcelain of the sixteenth century displays the native character and has simple designs in blue covering only a small area of the surface. The reason for this probably is that the imported cobalt was preferred on account of its bright colour, but it was too costly to be used in large quantities.

After the Japanese invasion and until the middle of the eighteenth century blue designs were applied sparingly to conserve the valuable cobalt. In 1754 King Yŏngjo prohibited the use of blue-and-white porcelain by the common people, indicating that the wares were regarded as luxury products at that time. However, white porcelain with underglaze iron-brown decoration was produced extensively and doubtless was in general use. By the nineteenth century blue-and-white was again being produced in quantity, and the blue pigment was freely used. Many fine specimens of writer's accessories — brush stands, brush washers, water pots, etc. — were made at the Punwŏn kilns. However, the blue colour is not clear-cut, the quality of the clay had become coarser and there was a tendency towards excessive decoration. As mentioned earlier, the Punwŏn kilns were becoming less active as the nineteenth century wore on, and the tradition of Korean blue-and-white gradually failed.

(4) White Porcelain with Underglaze Iron Decoration

This class of ware probably was made in the first period, although most of the surviving examples are believed to be products of the second. It is characterized by swift, free brushwork and is unsurpassed in vigour and artistry. The wares were produced for the most part at private kilns in northern Korea, and the animals, trees, etc. depicted on them bear witness to the talent of a native school of potter-painters whose work is quite distinctive.

(5) White Porcelain with Underglaze Copper Decoration

Copper-red was used by itself to paint designs. There are also some examples where copper-red and blue were used together. The history of underglaze copper decoration in Korean ceramic art goes back to the Koryŏ period. Most of the Yi period white porcelains with copper-red designs belong to the second period and are thought to have been made at the Punwŏn kilns.

(6) MISCELLANEOUS WARES WITH COLOURED GLAZES

There are also various minor products with black, yellowish brown, azure and opaque glazes. These were all made at provincial potteries in different parts of Korea.

NOTES AND PLATES

2

JAR

Grey stoneware; Silla dynasty; 5th/6th century
Ht. 40 cm. From Kyŏngju region
National Museum of Korea

This jar with its tall cylindrical neck and openwork foot represents one of the most popular types of vessel made in the Silla period. The mouth-rim is bevelled to enable a cover to fit easily. Round the shoulder of the jar is a crudely incised design of five horses, and there are two bands of vertical combed decoration round the neck and another round the body. It is thought that the horse design may not have been purely decorative but had some magic significance. The openwork foot is characteristic of Silla pottery during the first period (*c.* A.D. 380–600).

C

3

POTTERY VESSEL IN THE FORM OF A MOUNTED WARRIOR

Grey stoneware; Silla dynasty; 5th/6th century
Ht. 24 cm. Excavated from the 'Gold Bell Tomb' Kyŏngju
National Museum of Korea

This pottery figure of a mounted warrior is a remarkable relic of Old Silla. The horseman wears full military dress, consisting of a pointed hat, jerkin and rectangular leg-guards — probably made of leather; the hat, perched somewhat precariously, is fastened by a chin-strap. Man and horse were fashioned separately, the latter being hollow and having a tubular spout projecting from its chest and a cup-shaped funnel surmounting its rump: thus the figure could serve as a pouring vessel, though it is unlikely to have been so used owing to its weight and the difficulty of handling.

Though less spirited than the Chinese T'ang figures, this splendidly symbolic representation achieves great force; the elaborate armour and trappings help to create an impression of strange, archaic dignity.

4

CUP WITH COVER

Grey stoneware; Silla dynasty; 5th/6th century
Ht. 15 cm. From Kyŏngju region
National Museum of Korea

The covered cup with openwork foot is the commonest of all
Silla vessels, comprising about half the pottery wares found in the
tombs around Kyŏngju. It was used, not as a drinking cup, but to
contain food. It consists of a shallow bowl mounted on a tall,
conical foot with two rows of rectangular openings together with a
cover surmounted by an openwork knob, which serves as a foot
when the cover is removed and turned over. There is a band of
vertical combed decoration round the cover: other examples have
several such bands.

5

BURIAL URN

Earthenware covered with an olive glaze; Silla dynasty; 8th/9th century
Ht. 25 cm. From Kyŏngju region
National Museum of Korea

This type of vessel was used to hold the ashes of the dead after cremation in accordance with Buddhist custom. A large covered jar with short neck and foot, it has four animal-mask handles on the shoulder. The whole surface is covered with bands of stamped rosettes, quatrefoils, lozenges, discs and 'rice-grain pattern' — characteristic of the later Silla pottery from the seventh century onward. Burial urns of this type, both glazed and unglazed, are found in considerable number in the Kyŏngju region.

6

JAR

Porcellanous stoneware with pre-celadon glaze; Koryŏ dynasty: A.D. 993
Ht. 35·2 cm. Diam. 20 cm.
Present owner unknown

This jar is the earliest known Koryŏ ware with a celadon type glaze. The body is greyish brown and is covered with an olive glaze having fine, close-meshed crazing. On the base is an incised inscription reading as follows: 'Made in the fourth year of Soon-hwa (the Sung era *Shun-hua*), the year Ke-sa (*Kuei-ssŭ* in Chinese, corresponding to A.D. 993), for use in the First Room of the Shrine of King T'aejo, by the potter Choi Kil-hwoi.'

The style and glaze of this jar show that it is one of the earliest pieces made during the long development of celadon ware. It shows some likeness to the Chinese Yüeh celadons of the Five Dynasties period.

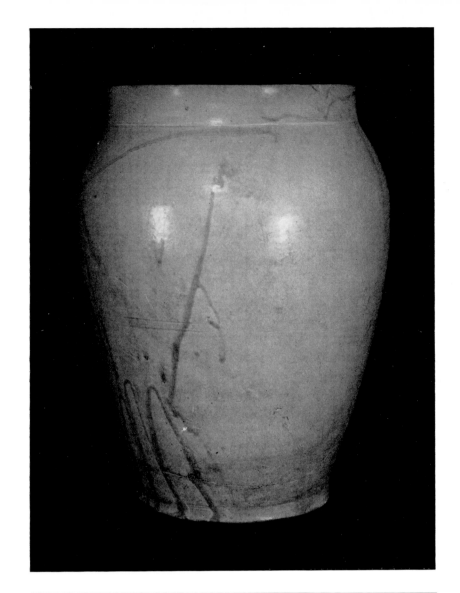

7

VASE

Celadon ware; Koryǒ dynasty; 11th/12th century
Ht. 24·4 cm. Diam. (max.) 13·4 cm.
National Museum of Korea

The simple form of this vase is set off by four loop handles placed just above the shoulder and decorated with chrysanthemum reliefs at their junction with the body. The light grey body is covered with a smooth, pale celadon glaze without crazing.

8

INCENSE BURNER

Celadon ware; Koryŏ dynasty; 12th century
Ht. 15·1 cm. Diam. at mouth 12·3 cm. Diam. at base 8·8 cm.
Duksoo Palace Museum of Fine Arts

This urn-shaped incense burner with flaring mouth was made in two sections joined together with a thickly modelled ring. It has a band of carved lotus petals, pointing upwards, round the body and another band, pointing downwards, round the base. The glaze is a smooth bluish green.

9

INCENSE BURNER WITH MANDARIN DUCK COVER

Celadon ware; Koryŏ dynasty; 12th century
Ht. 21·6 cm. Width 16·8 cm.
Collection of Mr Hyung-pil Chun

This incense burner has a cover surmounted by a seated Mandarin Duck, modelled in the round. The body of the duck is hollow to allow the incense smoke to emerge from its open bill. The eyes are marked with underglaze iron and the feathers are incised. The sides of the bowl and base of the cover are incised with waves and arabesques. The vessel is supported by three lion-headed feet. The glaze is pale green with some crazing, but the head and neck of the duck are slightly browned by oxidation.

10

INCENSE BURNER WITH
LION COVER

Celadon ware; Koryŏ dynasty; 12th century
Ht. 21·5 cm. Width 16·3 cm.
National Museum of Korea

This incense burner has a cover surmounted by a lion, modelled in the round, seated with one forefoot gripping a ball. The wide-rimmed bowl of the incense burner rests on three lion-headed feet. The body of the lion is hollow to allow the incense smoke to emerge from its open mouth. The eyes are marked with underglaze iron; a bell hangs round its neck; the large flat tail is turned up its back and the mane and other features are shown by incising. The sides of the bowl are decorated with incised cloud or wave patterns, and the flat rim — likewise the base of the cover — with flowers and stylized clouds. The glaze is a fresh green colour, but there are some bare spots where the body has not been covered and has turned brown in the course of firing. A vessel of this kind is described by Hsü Ching, the Chinese scholar who visited Korea with the Sung envoy in 1123: he was greatly impressed by its novel design and beautiful celadon glaze.

II

INCENSE BURNER WITH CH'I-LIN COVER

Celadon ware; Koryŏ dynasty; 12th century
Ht. 17·6 cm. Width 16 cm.
Duksoo Palace Museum of Fine Arts

This incense burner has a cover surmounted by a *ch'i-lin* —
a mythical beast something like the unicorn of Western fable —
modelled in the round. The beast is seated with open mouth, from
which the incense smoke could rise through the hollow body. The
eyes are marked with underglaze iron and the mane and other
features are incised. The edge of the cover is decorated with
incised key-fret pattern, above which are stylized clouds. The
vessel is supported by three lion-headed feet. The glaze is a pale
greyish green.

12

WATER POT IN THE FORM
OF A FISH-DRAGON

Celadon ware; Koryŏ dynasty; 12th century
Ht. 24·5 cm. Diam. of body 13·5 cm.
National Museum of Korea

This is a water or wine pot in the form of a fish-dragon. The dragon's head forms the spout and its upraised tail serves as a cover. Two large fins shaped like wings rest on either side of the scaly body: head, fins and tail are modelled and have incised detail with touches of white slip under the glaze. From the twisted lotus-stem handle depend two lotus buds and leaves, and the base is encircled by overlapping lotus petals. The glaze is a lustrous green.

According to the Chinese legend, certain fish used to ascend the Yellow River, fight their way through the cataracts and finally leap the *Lung Mên*, Dragon Gate. If they succeeded in passing this, they were transformed into dragons.

13

WATER POT IN THE FORM OF A DRAGON-HEADED TORTOISE

Celadon ware; Koryŏ dynasty; 12th century
Ht. 17·3 cm. Length 20·2 cm.
Duksoo Palace Museum of Fine Arts

This vessel is in the form of a dragon-headed tortoise seated on a lotus pedestal with overlapping petals. The dragon-head forms the spout, and a lotus leaf modelled on the back with a hole in the centre provides an opening through which to pour liquid into the pot. No doubt a stopper in the form of a lotus bud was originally included, as seen in other examples. The head and body are modelled; incised detail was added, especially the hexagonal markings on the tortoise's shell; spots of underglaze iron also ornament the twisted lotus-stem handle. The glaze is a lustrous bluish green, especially where it has pooled thickly; elsewhere it is a paler greyish green.

Some tortoises were believed to possess dragon qualities and were often portrayed with dragon-heads; chief of these was the 'Divine Tortoise' which had attained the age of one thousand years.

14

INCENSE BURNER WITH OPENWORK BALL COVER

Celadon ware; Koryŏ dynasty; 12th century
Ht. 15·5 cm. Diam. at centre 10·1 cm.
Duksoo Palace Museum of Fine Arts

This elaborate incense burner has been justly called a *tour de force* of the potter's art. The cover is in the form of a ball with a reticulated openwork pattern mounted on a foliate base with a hole in the centre to enable the incense smoke to rise and disperse through the apertures in the ball; at the intersections of the interlocking circles spots of white slip are painted under the glaze. The bowl of the incense burner is encircled by four rows of modelled petals with serrated edges and incised veins; this rests on five large down-turned petals, also modelled and turning up at the tips. Beneath is a foliate base supported by three feet modelled in the form of rabbits, with spots of underglaze iron to mark the eyes. The glaze is a soft bluish green. A wide potter's crack runs across the base.

15

WATER DROPPER IN THE FORM OF A DUCK

Celadon ware; Koryŏ dynasty; 12th century
Ht. 8 cm. Length 12·6 cm.
Collection of Mr Hyung-pil Chun

Water droppers for use in calligraphy are not uncommon among Koryŏ celadons, but most of them are in the form of small jars or vases. Some rare examples of human or animal figures have survived, modelled in the round: this one of a duck is among the most accomplished and charming. The eyes are marked with underglaze iron and the feathers are delicately modelled and incised. On the back is a lotus leaf with a hole in the centre to admit water; the stopper is in the shape of a lotus bud. The duck holds a twisted lotus stem in its bill: this is looped on the far side — not visible in the illustration — to form a spout, but the spout itself is missing.

16

WATER DROPPER IN THE FORM OF A MONKEY HOLDING ITS YOUNG

Celadon ware; Koryŏ dynasty; 12th century
Ht. 9·8 cm. Width 6 cm.
Collection of Mr Hyung-pil Chun

Several water vessels in the form of ducks have survived, like the one shown in the preceding plate, and a few in the form of monkeys. Among the latter this unique example of a monkey with its young is the most pleasing. Specially noteworthy is the naturalism shown by the monkey's expression and the way in which the young one is touching its parent's face with its hand. The eyes and noses of the two monkeys are marked with underglaze iron spots, and there are holes in both their heads for admitting and dispensing water. The glaze is a fine green.

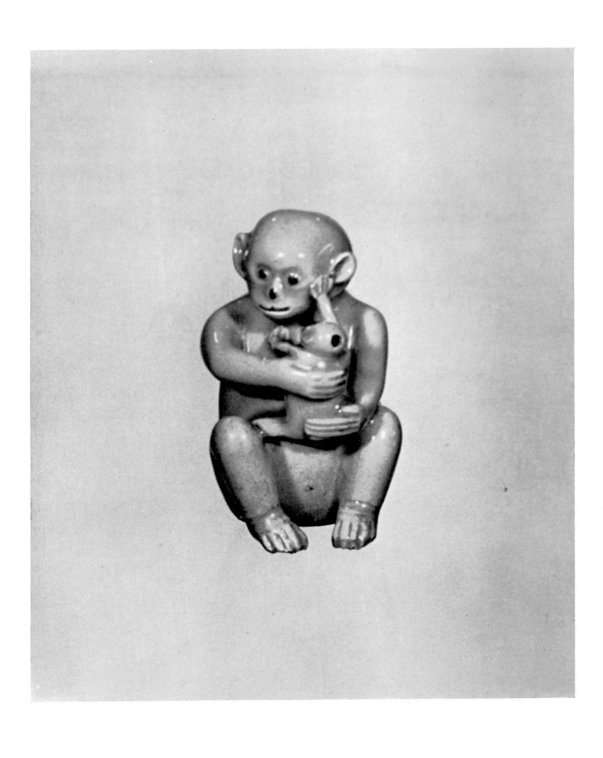

17

WATER POT IN THE FORM OF A MONKEY HOLDING A BOWL

Celadon ware; Koryŏ dynasty; 12th century
Ht. 7·1 cm.
Duksoo Palace Museum of Fine Arts

This is another example of a water vessel for use in calligraphy which takes the form of a monkey. The water was spooned out as required from the bowl. On the back of the grinning monkey is a bell, and its hairy body is indicated by incised lines; the eyes are marked with underglaze iron.

18

WATER DROPPER IN THE FORM OF A LOTUS BUD

Celadon ware; Koryŏ dynasty; 12th century
Ht. 10·2 cm. Diam. of base 4·6 cm.
National Museum of Korea

This water dropper takes the form of a miniature wine pot shaped like a lotus bud with a twisted vine handle. The veins are incised, and the edges of the petals are marked with spots of white slip under the glaze.

19

WATER POT AND COVER

Celadon ware; Koryŏ dynasty; 12th century
Ht. 30·3 cm. Diam. of body 14·1 cm.
National Museum of Korea

This ewer has an unusual and elaborate cover; in fact the cover is
about the same height as the body of the ewer but is balanced by the
relatively large spout and handle. The body is divided into vertical
ribs or lobes which are continued up the lower part of the cover.
Each rib is decorated with roughly incised arabesques. The spout is
hexagonal, and incised leaves round the lower part suggest a growing
shoot. The cover takes the form of a water-fowl with upraised wings
modelled on a triple lotus pedestal; at one side of this is a small loop
through which a cord or fibre could be passed to connect with a
similar loop, now broken, on the handle. The glaze is dark olive as a
result of oxidation in the firing.

20

WINE BOTTLE

Celadon ware; Koryŏ dynasty; 12th century
Ht. 28·2 cm. Diam. 14·2 cm.
Collection of Mr Hyung-pil Chun

This wine bottle with slender neck and flaring mouth is decorated in low relief as well as by incising. There is a band of stylized clouds round the mouth and a band of *ju-i* sceptre-heads round the shoulder, both in relief, as well as scattered cloud shapes on the body; the base is encircled by incised overlapping lotus petals. The glaze is pale bluish green with heavy striated and mesh crazing.

21

PRUNUS VASE

Celadon ware; Koryŏ dynasty; 12th century
Ht. 43·9 cm. Diam. of base 15·8 cm.
Duksoo Palace Museum of Fine Arts

This tall vase of baluster shape is widely known by the Chinese name *mei-p'ing*, and in Korean it is called *mae-pyŏng*, both signifying prunus vase. It is one of the favourite Koryŏ vessel forms, well suited to the display of a single branch of prunus blossom. The Korean type shows some difference from the Chinese, usually bulging more at the shoulder and tapering to the foot in a graceful curve with a slight return at the bottom. The decoration here is lotus blossoms and leafy arabesques incised over the whole body with an exceptionally thick line; round the base is a band of key-fret pattern. The glaze is a rich dark green.

This is one of the largest prunus vases ever found in Korea.

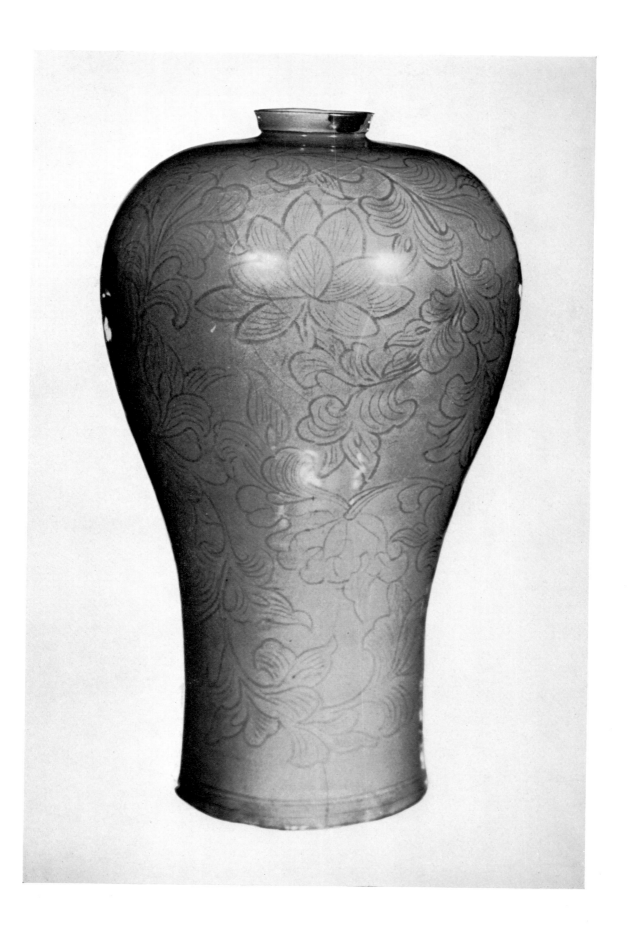

22

LOBED VASE

Celadon ware; Koryŏ dynasty; first half of the 12th century
Ht. 22·8 cm. Diam. at base 8·8 cm.
Excavated from the tomb of King Injong (reigned 1123–46)
National Museum of Korea

The eight-lobed form of this vase is that of an elongated melon, a *motif* completed by the mouth shaped like an eight-petalled melon blossom. The slender neck is divided by three incised lines, and the foot is strongly carved with overlapping flutings. The glaze is a quiet bluish green.

The vase was found in the tomb of King Injong, located near Kaesŏng. As King Injong died in 1146, it is likely that the vase was made at, or shortly before, this date. Thus, it is one of the few important 'documents' available for dating Koryŏ celadon ware.

23

WINE POT AND COVER

Celadon ware; Koryŏ dynasty; 11th/12th century
Ht. 18·5 cm. Diam. 14·5 cm.
National Museum of Korea

A favourite Koryŏ vessel was the melon-shaped wine pot. This example has a ten-lobed body, and its cover likewise is formed in ten petals. The handle is shaped like a twisted vine and has a small loop at the top from which the cover could be secured by a cord or fibre. The glaze is a pale green with striated crazing.

24

EWER WITH COVER AND BOWL

Celadon ware; Koryŏ dynasty; 11th/12th century
Ht. of ewer with cover 27·5 cm. Diam. of ewer 14·4 cm. Diam. of bowl 18·7 cm.
Duksoo Palace Museum of Fine Arts

The wide, flat-shouldered body of the ewer is surmounted by a cylindrical neck with an elaborate cover, consisting of a modelled lioness and her cub crouching on a lotus bud with a pedestal of two bands of lotus petals. There is a spout on one side, projecting vertically from the flat shoulder, and a handle joining the neck to the body on the other. The ewer fits snugly into a deep, six-lobed bowl. The form at once recalls that of Northern Sung ewers with bowls, notably a *ying-ch'ing* example in the British Museum. The glaze is a rich bluish green. The body is exposed along the lower edge of the cover and the foot of the bowl and has turned brown in the course of firing.

25

WATER POT AND COVER

Celadon ware; Koryŏ dynasty; 11th/12th century
Ht. 29 cm. Diam. of base 15·5 cm.
National Museum of Korea

This water pot is in the form of a lotus bud and has four rows of overlapping petals incised round the body. The handle is shaped like a twisted lotus-stem, and the cover is in the form of an inverted lotus flower with incised veins. The glaze is bluish green with striated crazing on the neck and mesh crazing round the lower part of the body, both stained yellow by impregnation with soil.

26

WINE CUP AND STAND

Celadon ware; Koryŏ dynasty; 12th century
Ht. 9·4 cm. Diam. of stand 14·7 cm.
National Museum of Korea

The eight-lobed wine cup with scalloped lip and foot is supported
by a stand with a wide flat rim and a central pedestal encircled with
carved lotus petals. The cup has a band of incised arabesque just
below the lip and an incised chrysanthemum spray on each lobe;
similar sprays are incised on each lobe inside, and at the bottom is an
incised chrysanthemum. The stand has eight indentations round the
edge, each lobe being decorated with incised chrysanthemum
sprays; between the pedestal and the rim is a depressed zone
decorated with incised fishes among waves. The pedestal has an
incised chrysanthemum flower at its centre. The foot of the stand is
lobed and scalloped, with incised floral decoration on each lobe.
The glaze is a fine bluish green.

27

BOWL

Celadon ware; Koryŏ dynasty; 11th/12th century
Ht. 5·5 cm. Diam. 18 cm.
Duksoo Palace Museum of Fine Arts

This bowl is decorated with a moulded design of boys playing in a pond among lotus plants and reeds together with Mandarin Ducks and geese. At the centre is a fish among waves. The bowl is undecorated outside, but the edge has six indentations. The glaze is bluish green without crazing.

28

PRUNUS VASE

Inlaid celadon ware; Koryŏ dynasty; 12th/13th century
Ht. 29 cm. Diam. of base 15·2 cm.
National Museum of Korea

This *mae-pyŏng* vase is remarkable for a combination of incised
and inlaid decorative *motifs*, the latter having the semblance of a
square cloth cover spread over the shoulder with tassels hanging
from the four corners. The edge of this simulated cloth cover and
the tassels depending from it are decorated by a beading of white
circles with black centres; within this border is a band of leaf
pattern enclosing chrysanthemum flower-heads in white and leaves
in black. The edge of the small mouth also is inlaid with key-fret
pattern in white.

Incised into the body are four tall peony sprays, evenly spaced
and separated by the inlaid pendant tassels already mentioned.
Round the base is an incised band of key-fret, above which incised
fungus patterns mount up towards the inlaid tassels. The whole
design is well conceived and deceptively simple in appearance.
The glaze is a subdued bluish green.

29

WINE POT AND COVER

Inlaid celadon ware; Koryŏ dynasty; 12th century
Ht. 21·5 cm.
Duksoo Palace Museum of Fine Arts

This is another example of the melon-shaped wine pot, similar to the one shown in Plate 23 but elongated in form and decorated with fine inlaid designs. It has eight lobes, the three each side inlaid in black and white with a lotus spray between two chrysanthemum sprays. The lobing is continued on the small cover, at the top of which is a looped stem encircled by melon seeds in relief; this stem could be connected with a small loop on the handle. Round the mouth and base are bands of lotus petals inlaid by the reverse method — the white inlay forming the background for a celadon pattern (this will henceforth be termed 'reverse inlay'). The glaze is a fine bluish green with some crazing. The tall, slender form of this wine pot and its delicate inlaid designs give an impression of refinement much to Korean taste.

30

WINE CUP AND STAND

Inlaid celadon ware; Koryŏ dynasty; 12th century
Ht. 10·3 cm. Diam. of stand 10·5 cm.
Collection of Mr Hyung-pil Chun

The wine cup is in the form of an eight-lobed flower and is supported by an ornamental stand with a pedestal in the centre; the stand is circular and has five feet with a raised edge and scalloped borders. The zone between the pedestal and the raised edge is decorated with five inlaid chrysanthemums, and the wine cup also has an inlaid chrysanthemum spray on each lobe. Inside the cup a peony spray is incised on each lobe. The glaze is pale green with some crazing on the cup.

31

SPITTOON OR SLOP-BASIN

Inlaid celadon ware; Koryŏ dynasty; 12th century
Ht. 9·8 cm. Diam. 22·1 cm.
Duksoo Palace Museum of Fine Arts

The exact use of this type of vessel in the Koryŏ period is uncertain. In recent years it has served as an ash-tray or spittoon, but it may have been used formerly as a slop-basin for receiving the dregs of wine cups at a dinner party. The globular body is decorated with three inlaid chrysanthemum sprays; the wide, bowl-shaped rim likewise has three inlaid chrysanthemum sprays underneath, and its top surface is decorated with a band of chrysanthemum heads near the edge and eight larger chrysanthemum sprays spaced evenly round the side, all inlaid. The glaze is bluish green without crazing.

32

BOWL

Inlaid celadon ware; Koryŏ dynasty; mid-12th century
Ht. 6·1 cm. Diam. 17 cm. Excavated from a tomb with an epitaph dated 1159
National Museum of Korea

This bowl is decorated inside with elaborate reverse inlay in white (see description of Plate 29), a formal chrysanthemum head at the centre and floral arabesques on the side; below the rim is a scroll band. Five inlaid chrysanthemum sprays are evenly spaced round the outside of the bowl, but here the stems and leaves are black; above them is a scroll band in white, but a petal band round the base is black.

The bowl was found in a tomb with an epitaph bearing a date corresponding to 1159; it is thus the earliest dated inlaid celadon. However, the *sanggam* technique seems to have been fully mastered by this time, suggesting that its introduction may have been considerably earlier.

33

BOWL

Inlaid celadon ware; Koryŏ dynasty; 12th century
Ht. 8·5 cm. Diam. 20·1 cm.
National Museum of Korea

This bowl is decorated inside with four evenly spaced fruiting branches, either of lychee or pomegranate, and another at the centre; this frequent *motif* is here inlaid solely in white, and there is also a white scroll band below the rim. Outside there is a similar scroll band, with four small flying cranes alternating with four stylized clouds underneath; the lower half is covered with arabesques in reverse inlay. All the inlay is white, excepting the eyes, beaks, legs and tail-feathers of the cranes. The glaze is bluish green with profuse crazing.

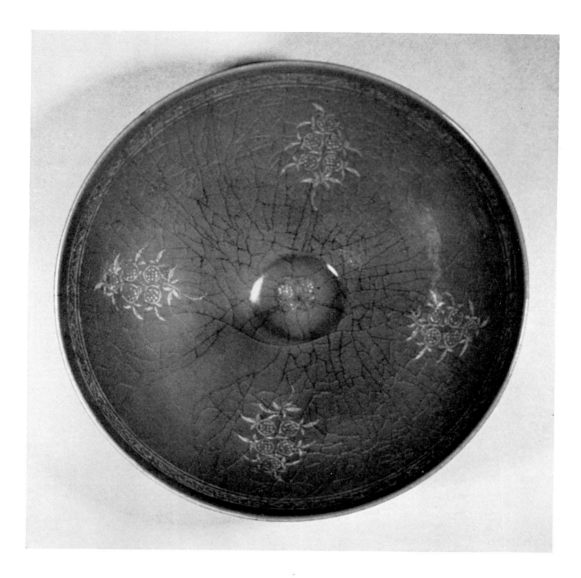

34

WATER POT WITH COVER
AND BOWL

Celadon ware; Koryŏ dynasty; 12th century
Ht. (together) 17·7 cm. Diam. of bowl 20 cm.
Duksoo Palace Museum of Fine Arts

The water pot and bowl were evidently made to go together. The body of the pot is covered with an openwork pattern of boys playing among lotus arabesques. The cover is decorated with incised clouds and key-fret pattern and surmounted by a figure, probably representing a Buddhist divinity, from which the head is missing. The bowl is encircled with three rows of overlapping lotus petals modelled in relief and having incised detail. The mouth-edge is ornamented with spots of white slip under the glaze. The glaze is partly oxidized and greyish brown in colour, but in places it is a rich green.

35

WATER POT IN THE FORM OF POMEGRANATES

Celadon ware; Koryŏ dynasty; 11th/12th century
Ht. 18·3 cm. Width 14·3 cm.
Duksoo Palace Museum of Fine Arts

This water pot is in the form of three pomegranates supporting a fourth. The handle is a stem connecting the top pomegranate with one of those underneath, and the spout is shaped like a pomegranate blossom. On the sides of the pomegranates are seed patches marked by spots of white slip under the glaze. Some leaves are attached to the stem forming the handle and to another stem at the side; details are incised. The glaze is a rich bluish green, darker in some parts and paler in others according to its density.

36

RITUAL EWER OR SPRINKLER

Inlaid celadon ware; Koryŏ dynasty; 12th century
Ht. 27 cm. Diam. of base 9·1 cm.
Collection of Mr Hyung-pil Chun

This is a type of vessel frequently encountered among Koryŏ wares, especially bronzes. It is believed to be a Buddhist ritual ewer or sprinkler. This example is inlaid with a design of willow-tree, reeds, lotuses and swimming Mandarin Ducks; on either side of the neck is a peony spray, and a band of *ju-i* sceptre-heads forms a collar round the base. All the inlay is white, with the exception of the ducks' eyes. The cover for the spout is missing. The glaze is a quiet bluish green.

37

PRUNUS VASE

Inlaid celadon ware; Koryŏ dynasty; 12th/13th century
Ht. 29·9 cm. Diam. of body 18·5 cm.
Duksoo Palace Museum of Fine Arts

This is one of the famous *mae-pyŏng* vases inlaid with flying cranes and clouds. The eyes, beaks and legs of the cranes are black, while their heads, necks, bodies and wings are white. They are portrayed in naturalistic and sometimes droll attitudes. The stylized clouds are all in white. Round the mouth-edge and also the foot are key-fret patterns in black. The glaze is a fine bluish green with profuse crazing.

38

BOWL

Inlaid celadon ware; Koryŏ dynasty; 12th century
Ht. 6.1 cm. Diam. 15.5 cm.
Duksoo Palace Museum of Fine Arts

This lovely bowl is remarkable for a combination of inlaid and relief decoration which rarely attained such perfection. Outside the bowl is undecorated, but inside there is an inlaid scroll band in white below the rim and an over-all moulded pattern of flowers and leaves with incised detail. The design is made more effective by the celadon glaze, which has run very thin over the relief pattern and pooled thickly round its edges, thus enhancing the plastic appearance of the floral decoration and making it almost as white as the inlay owing to the pale grey body showing through the glaze. The colour of the glaze is a rich bluish green with some crazing.

39

PILLOW

Inlaid celadon ware; Koryŏ dynasty; 12th century
Ht. 12·5 cm. Length 22·8 cm. Width 9·5 cm.
Duksoo Palace Museum of Fine Arts

This rectangular pillow is curved to form a concave rest for the head. The two wider faces are decorated with a central inlaid medallion of a crane flying among clouds; this is surrounded with reverse inlay arabesques. The two narrower faces have a central twelve-lobed panel within which are two peonies joined together by their stems; this likewise is surrounded with reverse inlay arabesques. The edges of the pillow at both ends have bands of overlapping lotus petals outlined in white and black, also in the reverse inlay technique, with half-chrysanthemum heads in white at the base of the front petals. The twelve-lobed panel *motif* is repeated at the ends of the pillow, with a round hole through the body at the centre and reverse inlay arabesques all round. Most of the inlay is white, but the medallions and panels are outlined also in black, and the beaks, eyes, legs and tail-feathers of the cranes are black, as usual, together with the leaves and stems of the peonies. The glaze is a fine bluish green with some crazing.

40

ROUND COSMETIC BOX AND COVER WITH FIVE SMALL BOXES NESTED INSIDE

Inlaid celadon ware; Koryŏ dynasty; 12th century
Ht. 8·4 cm. Diam. 19·1 cm. Small round box: ht. 3·1 cm.; diam. 7·9 cm.
Crescent-shaped boxes: ht. 3 cm.; length 7·8 cm.
Collection of Mr Hyung-pil Chun

This cosmetic set consists of a large round box with a smaller eight-lobed box and four crescent-shaped boxes nested inside, the arrangement suggesting a flower encircled by leaves. The large outer box has elaborate inlaid decoration on the cover, consisting of concentric bands of arabesque — two of lotus and one of chrysanthemum — separated by white rings and black dots. In the centre is a chrysanthemum surrounded by four lunettes containing flowers. The edge of the cover is decorated with a key-fret band and the lower part of the box with a scroll band, both in white. The covers of the inner boxes are all decorated with inlaid peony sprays set within panels formed by black and white lines which follow the lobed shape of the boxes; the lower halves of the boxes are undecorated. As usual, the flowers are all inlaid in white and the leaves and stems in black. The glaze is greyish green with a subdued sheen like polished stone.

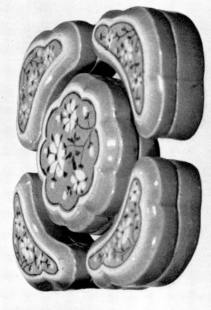

41

COSMETIC BOX AND COVER

Inlaid celadon ware; Koryŏ dynasty; 13th century
Ht. 3·4 cm. Diam. 9·4 cm.
Collection of Mr Jong-hwa Park

This cosmetic box is decorated with both inlaid and incised patterns. The cover has a chrysanthemum in the centre surrounded by five lunettes outlined in black and white; round these are two concentric bands of bead pattern in white and black separated by white rings: all this decoration is inlaid. Round the shoulder of the cover is an incised band of leaf arabesque. The lower half of the box has five stylized clouds incised along the edge within two incised rings, and the convex base is carved with fluting.

42

CYLINDRICAL BOX AND COVER

Inlaid celadon ware; Koryŏ dynasty; 12th/13th century
Ht. 5·9 cm. Diam. 7·8 cm.
National Museum of Korea

This type of box is believed to have been used as a tea-caddy or for medicine — at least two such boxes have been found inscribed with the name of the Government Medical Bureau. The sides of the box here shown are decorated with inlaid lotus arabesque, and the same theme is repeated on the cover in a broad band surrounding a central chrysanthemum and four lunettes, each containing a chrysanthemum; on either side of the lotus band is a ring of black dots, and the edge of the cover is fringed with chrysanthemums. As usual, the flowers are inlaid in white — the chrysanthemums having a black dot at their centre — and the leaves and stems in black. The glaze is greyish green.

43

OIL BOTTLE

Inlaid celadon ware; Koryŏ dynasty; 12th century
Ht. 3·4 cm. Diam. 8·1 cm.
National Museum of Korea

Numerous oil bottles of this type have been recovered from
Koryŏ tombs. They are believed to have been used for ladies' hair
oil and are often included among the vessels nested within a large
cosmetic box of the kind shown in Plate 40. This example has a
flattened body; others have a more globular shape. It is decorated
with three inlaid peony sprays, the flowers being in white and the
leaves in black. The glaze is pale bluish green, darker and greener
where it has pooled thickly inside the mouth.

44

OIL BOTTLE

Inlaid celadon ware; Koryŏ dynasty; 12th/13th century
Ht. 4·3 cm. Diam. 7·8 cm.
National Museum of Korea

This is another oil bottle, more globular in shape than the one shown in the preceding plate. The upper half of the body is decorated with an inlaid band of lunettes, each containing a chrysanthemum. Round the base is a band of lotus petals in reverse inlay with a white ground. The glaze is greyish green with some crazing.

45

COSMETIC BOX AND COVER

Inlaid celadon ware painted in underglaze copper and white slip;
Koryŏ dynasty; 13th/14th century
Ht. 2·7 cm. Diam. 7·3 cm.
National Museum of Korea

This is one of the rare pieces decorated with underglaze copper as well as inlay (see Plate 46 for a much finer example). It is a somewhat undistinguished round cosmetic box with a cover decorated with six chrysanthemums, the petals inlaid in white and the leaves in black; however, the centre of each flower is marked by a blob of cherry-red, the difficult copper oxide technique having met with unusual success. Round the sides are painted vertical stripes of alternate black and white under the glaze. The colour of the glaze is a dull greyish green, indicating a relatively late date of manufacture.

46

PRUNUS VASE

Inlaid celadon ware with underglaze copper ornament;
Koryŏ dynasty; 13th century
Ht. 34·8 cm. Diam of base 13·2 cm.
Duksoo Palace Museum of Fine Arts

This *mae-pyŏng* vase is one of the rare pieces decorated with underglaze copper as well as inlay. The copper is used to touch up the flowers and buds of three large peony sprays which form the main design on the sides of the vase; each spray consists of two flowers and a single bud inlaid in white. The stems and leaf-veins are black, but the leaves are outlined in white. A simulated cloth cover is inlaid round the mouth of the vase in scalloped or leaf-shaped form, with tassels hanging from the corners; its thick white border is outlined in black. Enclosed within are chrysanthemum sprays with white flower-heads and black leaves and stems. Round the foot is a band of key-fret pattern in black, above which are inlaid overlapping lotus petals with a double edge in white and scrolling veins in black.

The bold floral design requires broader treatment than usual and is made more effective by embellishment with underglaze copper; this should have become bright red but, as often the case with such early examples of this difficult technique, has turned a dark reddish brown. The celadon glaze is greyish green with some crazing.

47

LOBED VASE

Inlaid celadon ware; Koryŏ dynasty; 12th century
Ht. 25·6 cm. Diam of body 11·5 cm.
Duksoo Palace Museum of Fine Arts

This vase, like the one shown in Plate 22, has an eight-lobed body in the form of an elongated melon. The neck spreads out to form a foliate mouth. The tall splayed foot is strongly carved with fluting. The long neck is divided in the centre by two white rings, and each lobe of the body is decorated with alternate sprays of chrysanthemum and peony. At the base, just above the tall foot, is a band of overlapping lotus petals in reverse inlay. Round the shoulder is a band of *ju-i* sceptre-heads in white. All the decoration is inlaid, the leaves and stems of the flowers and edges of the lotus petals in black, the rest in white. At the base of the lotus petals are black spots ringed with white. The glaze is a lustrous bluish green faintly browned with oxidation on one side.

48

WATER JAR

Inlaid celadon ware; Koryŏ dynasty; 12th century
Ht. 19·7 cm. Diam. of base 14·8 cm.
Duksoo Palace Museum of Fine Arts

This is a grand pot, distinguished by its size and bold inlaid peony decoration. The handles on either side are attached to the body by finely modelled lions' heads, the ends of the handles being gripped in the lions' jaws. The peonies are inlaid in white, one on each side of the pot, with incised detail; the leaves are inlaid in black. The breadth of treatment and sharply contrasted colours against a grey-green background make this one of the most striking of the Koryŏ inlaid celadon wares. The glaze is a subdued greyish green, thinly but evenly coated over the body.

49

EWER AND STOPPER

Inlaid celadon ware; Koryŏ dynasty; 12th century
Ht. 34·6 cm.
National Museum of Korea

This is another favourite Koryŏ vessel in the form of a gourd. The graceful shape and balanced curve of spout and handle make it one of the most beautiful examples to have survived. The body is decorated with reverse inlay which as usual is in white and makes a fine contrast with the soft green arabesque of peony flowers and leaves. Reverse inlay in black is less common. The slender neck connecting the upper and lower parts of the gourd is faintly ribbed; three cranes flying among clouds are inlaid on the small upper section, the eyes, beaks, tail-feathers and legs in black, the wings and bodies in white, and above them is an inlaid petal band. Dotted lines of underglaze white slip are visible round the base of the spout and handle as well as on the spout itself. The glaze is a soft, milky green; a few small patches of the body are exposed and have turned brown in the firing.

50

FRAGMENT OF JAR

Inlaid celadon ware with overglaze gilt decoration; Koryŏ dynasty; 13th century
Ht. 25·5 cm. Width 20 cm.
National Museum of Korea

This large section of a jar was found early in 1933 near the site of the Koryŏ royal palace at Kaesŏng. It is decorated with an inlaid design of a monkey seated under a tree and holding a peach in its outstretched hand, the whole set within a quatrefoil frame surrounded with floral arabesques. Apart from the unusual nature of the design, this piece is remarkable for the addition of gilt decoration over the glaze, which has been found on only some half-dozen specimens of Koryŏ celadon. The gilding was employed here to point up the design and also, by itself, to provide supplementary detail; thus, a rock under the tree is traced in gold, and a gold line is drawn outside the inlaid frame. Most of the gold has worn off, leaving only an impression on the glaze, but in a few places it still shines brightly and adds lustre to the inlaid decoration. Enough remains of the far side of the vase to show that the inlaid design portrayed a hare seated under a tree.

The *Koryŏ-sa* or History of the Koryŏ Dynasty, records the use of gold for decorating porcelains during the reign of King Ch'ungnyŏl (1275–1308), and it is thought that this jar was made about that time. The glaze is greyish green and somewhat degraded.

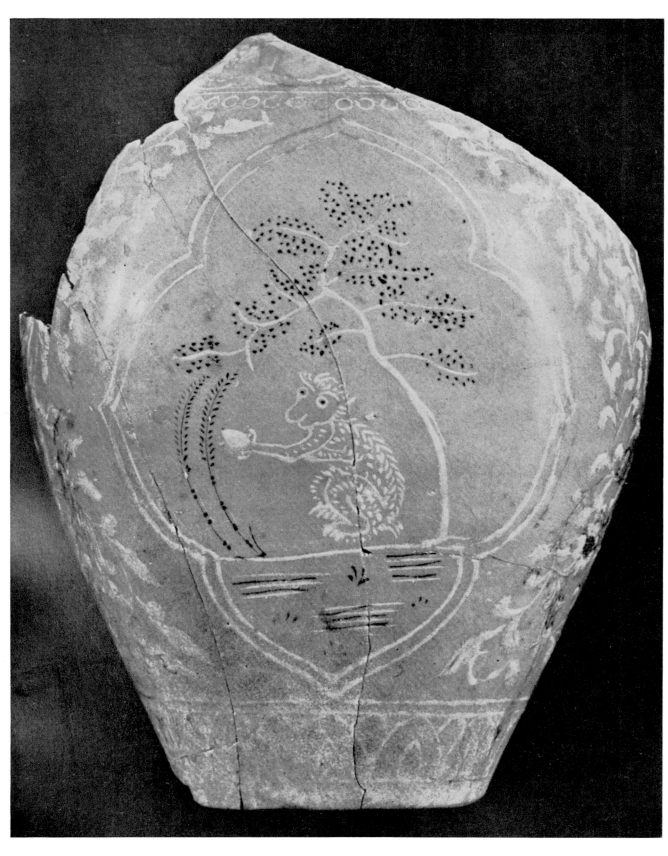

51

JAR WITH FLATTENED SIDES

Inlaid celadon ware; Koryŏ dynasty; 13th/14th century
Ht. 30·1 cm. Diam. of mouth 7·8 cm.
Collection of Mr Hyung-pil Chun

This type of jar with flattened sides was popular during the latter part of the Koryŏ period. However, the two animal-mask handles are unusual. The inlaid decoration is bold, though carelessly executed, consisting of quatrefoil frames enclosing lotuses, with birds perching on branches of flowering peach on either side. Round the shoulder and base are overlapping lotus petals, with a circlet of bead pattern level with the handles. The glaze is greyish green.

52

JAR WITH FLATTENED SIDES

Inlaid celadon ware; Koryŏ dynasty; 13th/14th century
Ht. 25·1 cm. Diam. of base 11·2 cm.
Duksoo Palace Museum of Fine Arts

This is another jar of the same type as the last but without handles. The inlaid quatrefoil frames here enclose a homely scene of a man outside a house (on the opposite side he is within the house), beside which flowers and bamboos are growing; there are two birds perched in the bamboos and two ducks in the foreground walking up from a pond. Round the shoulder and base are overlapping lotus petals, and the space between the frames is filled with floral arabesques. The inlaid decoration is mainly in white, but black is used also to give variety and point up the design. The glaze is greyish green, of uneven tone.

53

JAR WITH FLATTENED SIDES

Inlaid celadon ware; Koryŏ dynasty; 13th/14th century
Ht. 27 cm. Diam. of base 12·9 cm.
Collection of Mr Jai-hyung Sohn

This jar is elaborately decorated with inlaid quatrefoil frames and a simulated cloth cover round the shoulder, from which tassels depend. The design within the frame is a willow-tree, and on either side are tall, feathery reeds, above which flights of cranes are passing. Round the base is a band of overlapping lotus petals. The frames on both sides are bordered with white dots and the simulated cloth cover with bead pattern: this style of decoration, together with the tassels, is typical of the later inlaid celadons. The glaze is pale greyish green, and it is evident that chief attention has been given to the decorative features.

54

BOWL AND COVER
WITH STAND

Inlaid celadon ware; Koryŏ dynasty; 14th century
Ht. 20·4 cm. Diam. 19·3 cm.
Collection of Mr Hyung-pil Chun

Koryŏ vessels are often provided with stands which appear disproportionately small to our eyes. In this case a relatively large bowl with a dome-shaped cover is supported by a basin with wide, flat rim and small foot: the effect is somewhat top-heavy, although the shapes are conformable. This infelicity of form is matched by conventional inlaid decoration and an impoverished greyish glaze — all of which betoken the decline of Koryŏ celadon ware during the late thirteenth and fourteenth centuries.

The bowl is decorated inside with cranes flying among clouds and outside with four chrysanthemums set within roundels and surrounded with arabesques; above this is a band of stylized clouds, with key-fret pattern round the rim. The cover is decorated with bands of cranes flying among clouds, chrysanthemum heads and, at the top, lotus petals, each separated by double rings in white. The cover has a knob in the form of a *ju-i* sceptre-head.

55

PRUNUS VASE

Celadon ware painted in underglaze iron; Koryŏ dynasty; 13th century
Ht. 27 cm. Diam. of mouth 4·8 cm.
Collection of Mr Hyung-pil Chun

This *mae-pyŏng* vase is painted in iron under the glaze after the style of Chinese Tz'u-chou ware. The effect, however, is very different and characteristically Korean, while the glaze is light brown as a result of oxidation. The over-all floral design, however, is a thick, lustrous lacquer-black, and the condition of the glaze is extremely fine, with a rich surface gloss unimpaired by age or burial.

56

PRUNUS VASE

Celadon ware painted in underglaze iron; Koryŏ dynasty; 13th century
Ht. 26·7 cm. Diam. of base 9·5 cm.
National Museum of Korea

The graceful shape of this *mae-pyŏng* vase and the fine drawing of three floral sprays, with incised veins in sgraffiato style, make it one of the finest of its class. Decoration round the shoulder and base is omitted, leaving the floral sprays to produce their own restrained effect; the incised detail lightens the design and enhances the naturalism. The glaze is light brown as a result of oxidation.

57

JUG WITH COVER

Celadon ware painted in underglaze iron; Koryŏ dynasty; 13th century
Ht. 21·2 cm. Diam. of body 14·4 cm.
Duksoo Palace Museum of Fine Arts

Vessels of this shape are all decorated with underglaze painting and most of them seem to date from the thirteenth century. The wide cylindrical neck, ovoid body and graceful spout, balanced by a short handle, give them a familiar, practical appearance. The decoration is confined to a boldly painted peony in underglaze iron on either side, with some spots and splashes of black on the neck, spout and handle; a floral spray adorns the low, dome-shaped cover. The glaze is a murky grey-green, probably the result of the paste being impure and some degree of oxidation in the firing.

58

PRUNUS VASE

Celadon ware painted in underglaze iron; Koryŏ dynasty; 13th century
Ht. 36·6 cm. Diam. of base 11·3 cm.
National Museum of Korea

This is another *mae-pyŏng* vase painted in iron under the glaze. On the shoulder round the short neck is a wide band of chrysanthemum petals, and the body of the vase is covered with an overall pattern of chrysanthemum flowers entwined with leaf-sprays. Round the base is a solid band of black. The bold effect of the iron-black and the graceful, fluent drawing make this a striking piece; but the glaze is tinged with brown as a result of oxidation.

M

59

PRUNUS VASE

Celadon ware painted in underglaze slip; Koryŏ dynasty; 13th century
Ht. 30 cm. Diam. of base 12 cm.
Collection of Mr Hyung-pil Chun

Sometimes underglaze painting in slip was used for decoration instead of inlay, indeed it seems likely that this method was tried first of all but was superseded by the more complex technique of inlaying. However, it continued to be employed to some extent, especially for supplementary detail on inlaid wares, and finally it came back into more general use in the thirteenth and fourteenth centuries. This is one of the later examples with cranes flying among clouds painted in both black and white slip; the smudgy effect of the thick slip-painting is far removed from the delicacy of the inlay executed from the middle to the end of the twelfth century. The glaze is greyish green and shows some brownish oxidation.

60

PRUNUS VASE

Inlaid celadon ware; Koryŏ dynasty; 14th century
Ht. 29·2 cm. Diam. of base 10·5 cm.
Duksoo Palace Museum of Fine Arts

This is an exceptionally fine example of the inlaid ware produced in the late fourteenth century, when the decline of Koryŏ celadon had reached an advanced stage in transition to the *punch'ŏng* ware of the early Yi period. The decoration is profuse and stereotyped, the glaze pale grey. However, the design of four medallions, each containing two large fish, head to tail, is striking; it is set off by the surrounding cloud of white dots, with small cranes between each medallion. The scales of the fish are marked in white and their heads, eyes, fins and tails in black, while around them, inside the medallions, are black flecks symbolizing waves. The shoulder has a collar of lotus petals outlined in black and white, below which is a scroll band in white. Round the base of the vase are tall overlapping lotus petals in white. The contracted waist is typical of the late-fourteenth-century *mae-pyŏng* vases.

61

PRUNUS VASE

Inlaid white porcelain; Koryŏ dynasty; 12th/13th century
Ht. 28·8 cm. Diam. of base 10·5 cm.
Duksoo Palace Museum of Fine Arts

This celebrated white porcelain *mae-pyŏng* vase is unique in having inlaid decoration of a remarkably elaborate type. It is indeed a ceramic *tour de force*, but one that will not appeal to the taste of many, and it must be admitted that the technical skill of the potter has not been quite equal to his inventive power.

The vase is six-lobed and has a contracted waist; some distortion has resulted in the firing, and there is a pronounced kink on one side below the waist. Within each lobe is set a foliate panel, filled with the grey clay used in making celadon ware, and the use of a transparent glaze containing iron has converted these panels to a pale celadon colour. Inlaid within the panels are designs of willows, reeds, herons and peony sprays in black and white: some of the iron-black inlay has melted and run, showing brown and reddish blotches. Round the neck is a collar of chrysanthemum petals inlaid with grey clay — now pale celadon — and round the base a band of overlapping lotus petals executed in the same way but having borders carved in the white body. The transparent glaze shows a decided blue tone where it has pooled, especially round the base and along the indentations marking the lobes, but there are also patches of ivory tone caused by faint oxidation or burial.

Thus, against a background of white porcelain there is an inlaid celadon collar, inset celadon panels containing designs inlaid in black and white and an inlaid celadon lotus petal band round the base. Profuse crazing, both mesh and striated, covers the glaze; the body is very hard.

Some fragments of inlaid white porcelain have been excavated from the Yuch'ŏn-ni kiln-site on the west coast of Korea, but no other complete specimen decorated in this way is known.

[142]

62

INCENSE BURNER AND COVER

White porcelain; Koryŏ dynasty; 12th century
Ht. 8·5 cm. Diam. 8·1 cm.
Collection of Mr Hyung-pil Chun

This incense burner has a bluish white glaze similar to Chinese *ying-ch'ing* ware. Its cover is in the form of the Chinese 'hill-jar' covers for incense burners made in the Han period and has five openings round the side and one at the top to allow dispersion of the incense smoke. It is supported by three short feet.

The only Koryŏ kiln-site where white porcelain shards similar to this have been found is located at Yuch'ŏn-ni on the west coast, and it is probable that the incense burner, which was found in a tomb near Kaesŏng, was made at this place.

63

WINE CUP AND STAND

White porcelain; Koryŏ dynasty; 12th/13th century
Ht. 11·5 cm. Diam. of stand 13·2 cm. Ht. of cup 6·1 cm.
National Museum of Korea

Besides the Koryŏ white porcelain kiln-site located at Yuch'ŏn-ni on the west coast, white porcelain shards dating from the late Koryŏ and early Yi periods have been found near Yŏnghŭng on the east coast, north of Wonsan. However, there is at present very little information available concerning Koryŏ white porcelain kilns, and it is impossible to determine where individual specimens were made. In some cases it is difficult to distinguish Koryŏ white porcelains from the Chinese *ying-ch'ing* wares which were their models. The bluish tone of the glaze is very similar and the paste also resembles that of the Chinese wares. The stand for this cup is unusual in having an openwork pedestal and three pairs of holes through the foot.

64

PRUNUS VASE AND COVER

White porcelain; Koryŏ dynasty; 12th/13th century
Ht. 31·5 cm. Diam. 17·5 cm.
Duksoo Palace Museum of Fine Arts

The shape of this *mae-pyŏng* vase is closer to that of Chinese
prototypes in having a straight side from the shoulder to the base
instead of the usual waist and slight flaring out at the foot seen in
most Korean examples; however, its Korean origin is not in question, and it is possessed of singular beauty and grace, enhanced by
the smooth bluish white glaze and the absence of any decoration.
The cover is the normal type, though very few have been found with
Korean *mae-pyŏng* vases.

65

BOTTLE

Celadon ware painted in underglaze iron; Koryŏ dynasty; 14th century
Ht. 31·5 cm. Diam. 12 cm.
National Museum of Korea

This cylindrical bottle is painted in underglaze iron with a willow-tree design on either side. The straight wall of the body is bevelled at the top to meet the flat shoulder, out of which rises a short neck with flaring mouth-rim. The glaze is a warm brown as a result of oxidation except at the base, where it has a greenish tone.

The close relationship between Korean and Japanese wares of this period (late Koryŏ/earily Yi) is very marked. Many would say that this bottle has a 'Japanese' appearance; but this is mainly the result of strong Korean influence on Japanese ceramic wares and the adoption of Korean styles where these made a special appeal to Japanese taste.

66

BOTTLE

Celadon ware painted in underglaze slip; Koryŏ dynasty; 14th century
Ht. 26·1 cm. Diam. of mouth 8·9 cm.
Collection of Mr Hyung-pil Chun

This bottle shows the transition to Yi period style in full swing.
The abstract design painted under the glaze in white and black slip
is crudely executed, and the glaze is greyish green on one side but
brown on the other as a result of partial oxidation. The shape is
unusual and marks the trend away from the established tradition.

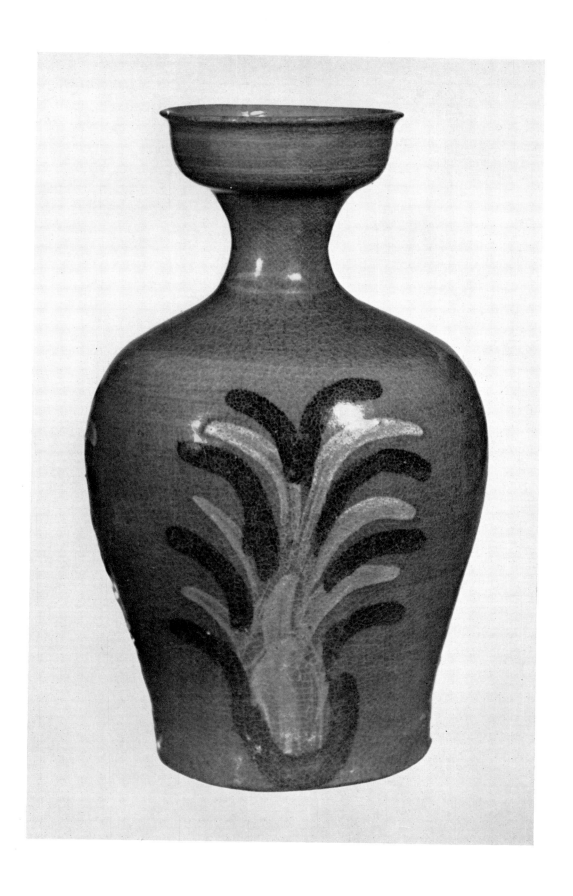

67

VASE

Iron-glazed ware; Koryŏ dynasty; 13th/14th century
Ht. 27 cm. Diam. of body 12·4 cm.
Duksoo Palace Museum of Fine Arts

This is an example of a strange and very uncommon ware produced towards the end of the Koryŏ period, in which a design was carved on the body and the background was cut or scraped away to allow it to be filled with white slip, somewhat after the manner of reverse inlay. The vessel was then covered with a glaze containing a high percentage of iron, with the result that the design stands out in rich brown while the background is a pale yellowish white. The decoration is striking but the effect somewhat crude.

The neck is decorated with stylized clouds, below which there is a band of overlapping lotus petals; at the junction of neck and body is a thick ring, from which vertical bands divide the body into five segments. In each segment is a peony spray with a *ju-i* sceptre-head at the apex. The lower part of the body is encircled with another band of overlapping lotus petals and is supported on a tall splayed foot. The iron glaze has lost its lustre but imparts a dark brown tone to the decoration and a paler tinge to the white background. Some fragments of this class of ware have been found at the Kangjin kiln-sites in south-west Korea.

68

PRUNUS VASE

Iron-black ware; Koryŏ dynasty; 13th century
Ht. 28·3 cm.
Formerly in the Collection of Mr Tai-shik Park

This is an example of another class of ware which was made during the latter half of the Koryŏ period; most of the surviving specimens are *mae-pyŏng* vases and this is one of the finest. The technique is unusual: first the body was coated with an iron pigment, then the design was painted in white slip and finally the vessel was covered with a transparent glaze of celadon type and fired. In this case the slip decoration takes the form of over-all floral arabesques. Fragments of this type of ware have been found at the Kangjin kiln-sites, and it is believed to have been introduced at the end of the twelfth century and to have been made chiefly in the thirteenth.

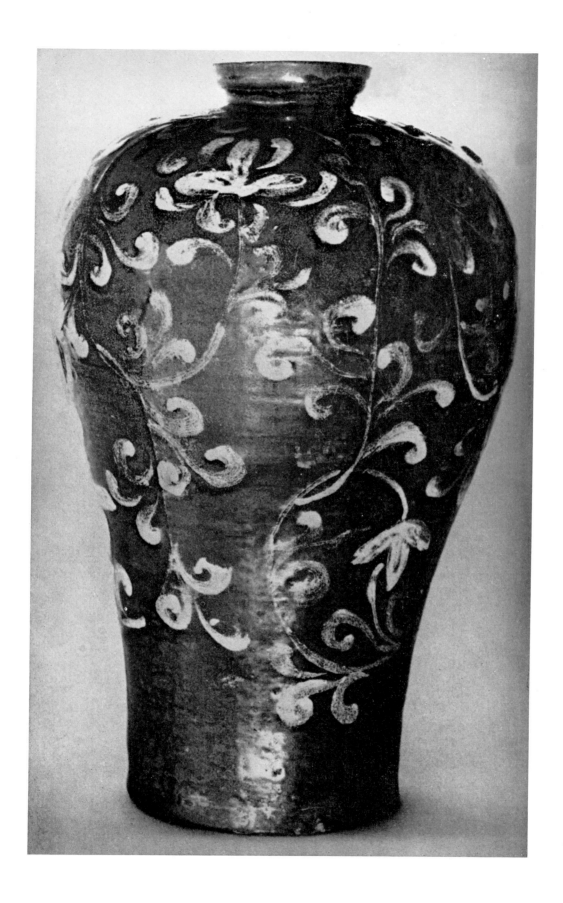

69

WINE BOTTLE

Inlaid celadon ware; Koryŏ dynasty; 14th century
Ht. 29·4 cm. Diam. of base 12·2 cm.
Collection of Mr Hyung-pil Chun

This is an unusual piece thought to have been sprayed with iron oxide before being glazed. The inlaid decoration has run into blotches, probably as a result of faulty firing. However, what would be considered blemishes in the West often have a special appeal in the Far East, where oddness is appreciated for its own sake and equated with character and pathos.

70

WINE FLASK

Punch'ŏng ware; Yi dynasty; 15th century
Ht. 20·7 cm. Width 16·9 cm.
Collection of Mr Hyung-pil Chun

This is a wine flask with flattened sides brushed unevenly with white slip and decorated with incised designs. On one side is a rough sketch of a bird, probably a crane, catching a fish; on the other is a man in a sailing-boat. A few other incised lines and vague patterns complete the decoration. The glaze is greyish green. Fragments of the same type of ware have been found at kiln-sites in south-western Korea.

71

BOTTLE

Punch'ŏng ware; Yi dynasty; 14th/15th century
Ht. 18·9 cm. Diam. at mouth 5·7 cm.
Taegu Municipal Museum

This bottle has a globular body with flattened sides and a small mouth. The paste is greyish white and the glaze a pale celadon. The decoration consists of inlaid floral and leaf designs with a background of stamped flower-heads inlaid in white.

Over-all patterns of flower-heads and other *motifs* are characteristic of the first part of the Yi period and have been known by the Japanese name *mishima*. They were produced by methods very different from the careful and intricate inlay of the Koryŏ potters, although they certainly derived therefrom. The designs were stamped into the body, after which white slip was brushed over the whole surface; the excess slip was then wiped off, leaving the pattern filled with the residue. In short, this was a hasty, superficial and mechanical way of producing inlaid decoration, and the result was not comparable with the earlier inlay: the pattern is often confused and the effect impaired by traces of the excess slip, which could not be entirely removed and have imparted a greyish white tinge to the whole vessel.

This is a transitional piece reminiscent of Koryŏ inlaid celadon but closer to the *punch'ŏng* ware of the Yi period. Similar examples are known to have been made at the Muan, Changheung and Kyŏngju kilns.

The term *punch'ŏng* is used in Korea to describe what the Japanese call *mishima* and *hakeme* (see Plate 83). It is the Korean rendering of the Chinese *fên ch'ing* signifying pale blue or green, and is appropriate in so far as the glaze is of celadon type, i.e. it contains iron and therefore has a tendency to assume a greenish or bluish tone when the vessel is fired in a reducing atmosphere. Most of the *punch'ŏng* wares have a faint bluish or greenish tinge arising from this cause.

[162]

72

WINE POT AND COVER

Punch'ŏng ware; Yi dynasty; 14th/15th century
Ht. 13·9 cm. Diam. 14·7 cm.
Collection of Mr Hyung-pil Chun

This wine pot is considered to be in the form of a Mandarin Duck, the spout representing the duck's bill, the curved handle its wings and the globular pot its body. The inlaid decoration of four inverted pomegranates depends from the mouth and is covered with white hatching known as 'straw-mat pattern'. From the base inlaid leaf designs spread upwards, and the lid is decorated with lotus petals. An opening in the knob on the lid would allow a cord to be passed through. The glaze is greyish and the paste somewhat coarse. This is another transitional piece with broadly conceived inlaid designs derived from the Koryŏ period but profuse white hatching and a greyish tone typical of Yi period *punch'ŏng* ware.

73

WINE BOTTLE

Punch'ŏng ware; Yi dynasty; 14th/15th century
Ht. 18·8 cm. Length 23·8 cm.
Collection of Mr Hyung-pil Chun

Wine bottles of this shape, which we associate with old-fashioned hot-water bottles, were not uncommon in the Yi period. This example is decorated with large inlaid designs of two fishes on either side; they are accompanied by a school of small fry and enclosed by roughly drawn panels. At one end of the bottle are overlapping lotus petals, at the other white hatching known as 'rope curtain pattern'. Four lotus petals are inlaid round the small mouth and covered with white hatching. The glaze is pale greyish green.

74

PRUNUS VASE

Punch'ŏng ware; Yi dynasty; 15th century
Ht. 28·3 cm.
Collection of Mr Taik-sang Chang

Here the declining influence of Koryŏ celadon ware has nearly reached its end. The bold peony design is inlaid, but the crudeness of the technique and the exaggerated waist and coarse paste show the impact of the new Yi period. A broad black band round the shoulder is another unusual feature, and the lotus petals round the neck are rough and crude. Vases of this type are said to have been found in tombs on Cheju (Quelpart) Island.

75

RICE BOWL AND COVER

Punch'ŏng ware; Yi dynasty; 15th century
Ht. (with cover) 16 cm. Diam. 16·8 cm.
Collection of Mr Hyung-pil Chun

Here the form and style are definitely of the Yi period; yet the technique follows that of the Koryŏ, though the inlay is broader and shallower. A fresh creative impulse is clearly evident. The top of the cover is flat and ornamented with a large peony. Round both cover and bowl are bold peony arabesques, with grass patterns along the rim. The inside is left plain. The paste is coarse and the glaze greyish with a hint of green.

76

WINE BOTTLE

Punch'ŏng ware; Yi dynasty; 15th century
Ht. 20·3 cm. Diam. 15 cm.
Collection of Mr Hyung-pil Chun

This wine bottle is covered with thinly brushed white slip, a technique which became popular in the early part of the Yi period. The decoration was effected in sgraffiato style by cutting away the slip to leave a pattern in white against the background of the body. The darkness of this background has here been enhanced by a dressing which has given it an intense green colour. The glaze is bright green with profuse crazing.

77

WINE FLASK

Punch'ŏng ware; Yi dynasty; 15th/16th century
Ht. 9·4 cm. Diam. 24·1 cm.
Duksoo Palace Museum of Fine Arts

This 'tortoise-shaped' wine flask is covered with brushed white
slip, the decoration being effected in sgraffiato style by cutting away
the slip to leave a peony pattern in white against a dark background.
The darkness of the latter has been intensified on the upper surface by
a dressing containing iron oxide. This has produced a greenish black
colour all round the design, setting it off with great clarity. The glaze
is pale greyish green.

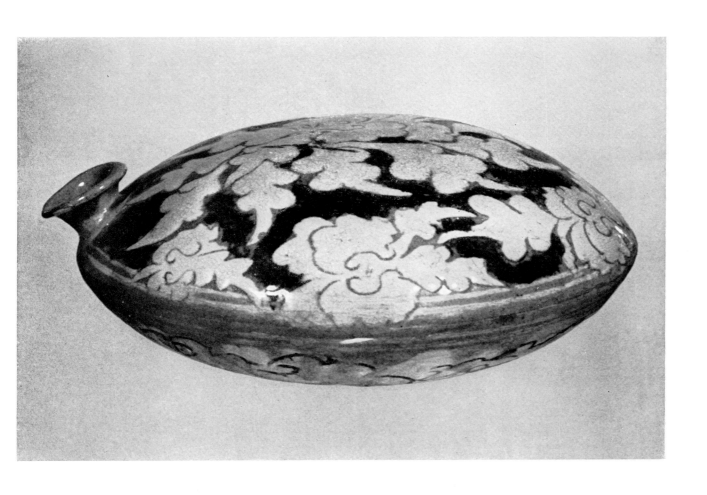

78

WINE BOTTLE

Punch'ŏng ware; Yi dynasty; 15th century
Ht. 32 cm. Diam. of base 8·5 cm.
Collection of Mr Hyung-pil Chun

This is another example of decoration in sgraffiato style, made by cutting away an over-all coating of white slip to leave the floral pattern standing out in white against the dark background of the body. The main pattern is a bold floral arabesque, but there is also a wide band of stylized petals round the shoulder. The base and top part of the neck with the flaring mouth are left plain. The glaze is pale green.

This is a type of ware produced at the Keryong-san kilns located at a mountain in central southern Korea, as well as at other potteries in southern Korea.

79

JAR

Punch'ŏng ware; Yi dynasty; 15th century
Ht. 15·5 cm. Diam. of body 19·9 cm.
Excavated from a kiln-site at Keryong-san in central southern Korea
National Museum of Korea

This fine jar with abstract decoration round the shoulder is typical of the wares made at the Keryong-san potteries, which were active from the beginning of the Yi period to the end of the sixteenth century. The jar was actually excavated from these kiln-sites in 1927. The decoration employed at the Keryong-san kilns is crude but charming and often remarkably modern in style. In this case the vessel has been covered with brushed slip and an arabesque design painted in iron under a glaze which has a yellow tinge.

80

WINE BOTTLE

Punch'ŏng ware; Yi dynasty; 15th/16th century
Ht. 29·2 cm. Diam. of body 17·9 cm.
Excavated from a kiln-site at Keryong-san in central southern Korea
Duksoo Palace Museum of Fine Arts

This is a fine example of the wares produced at the Keryong-san potteries, from which it was originally excavated. The grey body is covered with brushed white slip and decorated with an abstract design of two fishes, painted in underglaze iron. The naïve artistry with which this theme is treated heightens the effect: the fishes have fantastic but highly decorative fins; their scales are roughly indicated by rows of dots, and they seem to be playing with water-plants which they have seized in their mouths. The bottle is in fine condition, with a lustrous transparent glaze, in which there are some green 'tear-drops', and a faint green tone round the shoulder.

81

WINE FLASK

Punch'ŏng ware; Yi dynasty; 15th/16th century
Ht. 22·1 cm. Diam. of mouth 4·8 cm.
Duksoo Palace Museum of Fine Arts

The sides of this wine flask are slightly flattened to facilitate carrying. The body is covered with white slip, on which the marks left by the brush are clearly visible. The two sides are decorated with incised leaves and the ends with dots and geometrical patterns; round the shoulder is a broad band of chrysanthemum petals. The paste is coarse and the glaze tinged with brown.

82

WINE BOTTLE

Punch'ŏng ware; Yi dynasty; 15th century
Ht. 27 cm. Diam. of base 7·8 cm.
Duksoo Palace Museum of Fine Arts

This wine bottle is covered with stamped decoration known in
Korea as 'rope curtain pattern' and inlaid with brushed white slip.
A stamped ring of chrysanthemum heads encircles the neck just
above an undecorated band, and a similar chrysanthemum ring
appears on the foot. The glaze shows patches of discolouration but a
high gloss or lustre. This piece is typical of the ware called *mishima*
in Japan and was widely made in south-western Korea.

83

BOWL

Punch'ŏng ware; Yi dynasty; 15th century
Ht. 7·7 cm. Diam. 18·2 cm.
Duksoo Palace Museum of Fine Arts

This bowl is decorated outside with brushed white slip in the style called *hakeme* in Japan, while the inside is stamped with 'rope curtain pattern' and a petal band near the bottom. Two rings have been incised outside in sgraffiato style and several inside — four round the mouth-rim and one on either side of the petal band. Coarse brushing of white slip became a popular method of decoration in the early Yi period and was carried out with a miniature garden broom made of the grain ends of rice straw. The unselfconscious beauty of this style of decoration, as of Yi pots in general, has been much admired and has deeply influenced contemporary artist-potters in England and Japan.

84

BOWL

Punch'ŏng ware; Yi dynasty; 15th century
Ht. 8·2 cm. Diam. 19·7 cm.
National Museum of Korea

This bowl is decorated with stamped patterns over which white slip has been brushed to produce a type of inlay (see Plates 71, 82 and 83). The outside is stamped with 'rope curtain pattern' and several rings below the rim; the inside has bands of petals and a wide area of 'rope curtain pattern' with grass-like hatching round the rim.

85

WINE BOTTLE

Punch'ŏng ware; Yi dynasty; 15th century
Ht. 28·6 cm. Diam. of body 16·3 cm.
Collection of Mr Hyung-pil Chun

This wine bottle is similar in shape to the one shown in Plate 76, but the decorative technique is different. Here the same thinly brushed white slip covers the coarse grey body, but the lotus arabesque is painted in underglaze iron instead of being effected in sgraffiato; the leaves and background to the blossoms are heavily painted, but an arabesque band round the neck shows a lighter touch. The glaze has a green tinge; the decoration is dark brown. Probably this piece was made at the Keryong-san potteries.

86

BOWL

Punch'ŏng ware; Yi dynasty; early 15th century
Ht. 10·8 cm. Diam. 14·6 cm.
Collection of Mr Hyung-pil Chun

This lovely bowl with its pale brown colour and jet-black abstract decoration is believed to have been produced at the Keryong-san potteries early in the Yi period; fragments of similar type have been found at the kiln-sites.

The grey body is covered with a thin coating of brushed white slip, but a band round the rim was left bare and decorated with a rough incised pattern, inlaid with white slip. A floral arabesque is freely drawn in underglaze iron round the upper part of the body and crude lotus petals round the lower part. The interior of the bowl has been left plain. The foot is small but strongly cut. No doubt a cover was originally provided.

87

BOWL

White porcelain painted in underglaze cobalt; Yi dynasty; mid-15th century
Ht. 4·4 cm. Diam. 14 cm.
Collection of Mr Hyung-pil Chun

The technique of painting blue decoration under the glaze on white porcelain came into use in Korea during the fifteenth century: this is one of the earliest examples, notable for the fact that the characters *Chung Shik* have been inscribed on the base. These characters have been identified as the name of a personage who passed the national examination in the fourteenth year of King Sejong, corresponding to 1432, and subsequently gained high office in the Government. It is believed that the bowl was specially made for him in the latter half of the fifteenth century.

The decoration in cobalt blue round the outside of the bowl is sparing, confined to flowering plum branches, and shows the early use of the technique and scarcity of the material. Inside the bowl is decorated with lotus petals, also in cobalt blue, round the centre. The shape and style show strong influence from Ming China. The opaque blue decoration and free but unpractised hand of the painter are typical of the blue-and-white ware made at this period. Some small holes not visible in the illustrations occur at five places on the exterior: these are thought to have been made for fixing metal characters as additional ornament.

This bowl has come to light only recently and is an important 'document' — the earliest datable Yi porcelain with underglaze blue decoration.

88

BOTTLE

White porcelain painted in underglaze iron and cobalt;
Yi dynasty; 17th/18th century
Ht. 17·2 cm. Diam. 11 cm.
Collection of Mr Jai-hyung Sohn

This cylindrical bottle is an unusual shape. The creative power and vitality of the Yi potter is shown by the variety of shapes and styles of decoration employed. In this case the design of orchids, butterflies and dragonflies is painted in both underglaze iron-brown and cobalt-blue, the contrasting colours producing a pleasing effect. The white porcelain is heavily crazed and stained brown with age.

The close relationship between Korean and Japanese porcelain is shown by this example and some others which follow. Hundreds of Korean potters were settled in southern Japan after the Japanese invasion of 1592–8, and the earliest Japanese blue-and-white shows strong Korean influence. This has persisted to the present day, and leading contemporary artist-potters in Japan freely acknowledge their indebtedness to the Yi period craftsmen whose work excites so much admiration in their country.

89

JAR

White porcelain painted in underglaze iron; Yi dynasty; 17th/18th century
Ht. 30·8 cm. Diam. of base 16·4 cm.
National Museum of Korea

This celebrated jar is decorated in underglaze iron with four clusters of grapes; a naturalistic touch is added by a small monkey swinging on a vine. A decorative band encircles the short neck, and a rough, thick line the foot. The creamy glaze is covered with minute mesh crazing, which is stained brown with age on the lower part of the jar.

90

VASE

*White porcelain painted in underglaze cobalt; Yi dynasty; 17th/18th century
Ht. 25·6 cm. Diam. of base 11·6 cm.
Collection of Mr Hyung-pil Chun*

The shape of this vase is unusual, with wide mouth and swelling sides. The underglaze blue design is bold and free, showing a youth fishing among high rocks with orchids growing from them and two ducks approaching. The high quality of the porcelain and the painted design indicates that this may be a product of the official, or royal, potteries at Punwŏn, near Seoul.

91

JAR

Grey stoneware painted in underglaze iron; Yi dynasty; 17th/18th century
Ht. 36·4 cm. Diam. (max.) 28·6 cm.
Duksoo Palace Museum of Fine Arts

This round jar with its small mouth and foot is typical of the wares produced for general use at the numerous provincial potteries in Korea during the Yi period; they were mostly used as containers for food. The body is a relatively thin, hard stoneware and the decoration an abstract or impressionist sketch of a dragon flying above stylized clouds. The bold sweep of the brushwork and rich brown of the iron pigment produce an effect that evokes the admiration of modern artist-potters: here we see an example of the innate artistry of the peasant-potter, working with complete freedom to express his own concept of beauty in conditions of great hardship and poverty. According to Korean ideas, the dragon's position above the clouds shows that he is a 'full-fledged, heaven-called dragon'.

92

WINE BOTTLE

White porcelain painted in underglaze iron, copper and cobalt;
Yi dynasty; 17th/18th century
Ht. 42·4 cm. Diam. of body 22·9 cm.
Collection of Mr Hyung-pil Chun

This wine bottle conforms in general style to the type which was popular during the Yi period, but the slender neck and coloured decoration have become more familiar to us through Japanese porcelains, of which, however, the Korean bottles were the prototypes. The relief design of orchids and chrysanthemums is painted in iron-brown, copper-red and cobalt-blue, and the petals of one chrysanthemum have been left plain white; above the flowers are some butterflies, also in relief. Such variegated colouring is rarely seen in Yi period bottles, but the soft tones are in harmony and look well against the bluish white background. The glaze is covered with mesh crazing, stained brown with age on the neck and lower part of the body. The bottle is thought to be a product of the official Punwŏn kilns.

93

BOWL

White porcelain painted in underglaze cobalt; Yi dynasty;
early 19th century
Ht. 13·3 cm. Diam. 23·5 cm.
Collection of Mr Jai-hyung Sohn

This bowl is made of fine white porcelain decorated under the
glaze with a free design of flowering magnolia branches in pale
blue. The soft tone of the blue decoration is typical of Korean
blue-and-white and suggestive of a dreamy, poetical sensibility.
Just below the rim is a single ring of blue; a double ring marks the
lower edge of the floral design, and another ring encircles the foot.
The interior also is painted in underglaze blue with a floral *motif*
in the centre enclosed by a double ring.

An inscription in Korean script on the base is not clearly legible
but has been read as follows: 'This bowl was made in the year
Eul-mi for Court use.' This refers to the cycle which recurs every
sixty years, so that the date is uncertain but probably corresponds to
1835. However, the inscription may have been added at a date later
than manufacture.

94

JAR

White porcelain painted in underglaze iron; Yi dynasty; 18th/19th century
Ht. 30·7 cm. Diam. of base 11 cm.
National Museum of Korea

This jar was evidently made in two sections, an upper and a lower, which were luted together round the middle, where the body is slightly compressed. On both sides is a design of bare branches in underglaze iron. The glaze is ivory white with minute crazing. It is thought to have been made at a provincial kiln.

95

JAR

White porcelain painted in underglaze copper; Yi dynasty; 19th century
Ht. 29 cm. Diam. (max.) 23·5 cm.
Duksoo Palace Museum of Fine Arts

The shape of this jar, with its tall collar and wide shoulder tapering to a small foot, indicates that it was made in the latter part of the Yi period. There is a vague ring of underglaze blue just below the rim, but the main decoration is a flying phoenix on the front and back, boldly painted in underglaze copper. The swift brushwork and broad, abstract style of the design produce a powerful effect, standing out in dark red against a white background. The glaze is covered with mesh crazing and stained with age. The place of origin is not known but is thought to have been a pottery in the Kaesŏng/ Seoul region.

96

WINE BOTTLE

White porcelain painted in underglaze cobalt and copper;
Yi dynasty; 19th century
Ht. 32·2 cm. Diam. of body 20·5 cm.
Ehwa Women's University Museum

This is a typical wine bottle of the late Yi period, with tubular neck and broad base, a solid, satisfying shape which has the practical advantage that it is very difficult to overturn. The decoration is usually in underglaze blue, but this example is remarkable for a striking effect in dark red as well, produced by underglaze copper. The flowering plum branch is painted in both colours, and a broad band of copper traverses the design with a single bold brush-stroke. This vivid splash of colour across the conventional plum branch *motif* lends distinction, perhaps even a surrealist flavour, to an otherwise commonplace design and makes the wine bottle one of the most memorable of its type. The glaze is bluish white with striated crazing on the neck. The excellent technique indicates that it is probably a product of the official Punwŏn potteries.

97

WINE FLASK

White porcelain painted in underglaze cobalt; Yi dynasty; 18th/19th century
Ht. 18·1 cm. Width at base 8·1 cm.
Duksoo Palace Museum of Fine Arts

The flat, hexagonal body of this wine flask rests on an oval foot. Loops on either side are provided for a cord: by this means the flask could be slung round the neck on journeys or excursions. The blue decoration shows bees flying among carnations — on the opposite side there are only carnations — growing out of rocks; the flat edges are ornamented with stylized bats. The glaze is bluish white, discoloured grey on the foot.

98

WINE FLASK

White porcelain; Yi dynasty; 18th century
Ht. 21·7 cm. Diam. of body 18·4 cm.
Collection of Mr Hyung-pil Chun

This is another flask used for carrying wine or water on journeys or excursions. The form is simple but satisfying — a round body with flat sides, short neck and foot, in plain white without any decoration. The glaze is a soft greyish white with no crazing. The origin is unknown, but it is thought to show a sophisticated, urbane taste and may therefore have been made in the province of Kyŏnggi, around Seoul.

99

WATER DROPPER

White porcelain; Yi dynasty; 18th/19th century
Ht. 6·6 cm. Length 11 cm. Width 8·8 cm.
Collection of Mr Hyung-pil Chun

Water droppers for use in calligraphy are very numerous among Yi period wares, and many of them are of great charm; the majority are decorated in underglaze blue, but others have iron-brown or copper-red designs and some have been left plain. This example is rectangular and plain white, but there are two small modelled frogs, one on top and the other at the opposite end; their mouths are open to receive and dispense the water which the vessel was made to hold. There are triangular feet at the four corners. The purity of the bluish white glaze and refinement of the technique employed suggest that the piece may have come from the official Punwŏn potteries.

IOO

WATER DROPPER IN THE
FORM OF A DRAGON

White porcelain painted in underglaze iron and cobalt;
Yi dynasty; 18th/19th century
Ht. 12·8 cm. Width (max.) 12·1 cm.
Collection of Mr Hyung-pil Chun

This water dropper takes the unusual form of a dragon holding its pearl. The pearl and also the ridges along the dragon's spine are marked with underglaze iron, while details on the dragon's head, mane, etc., are picked out in underglaze blue. The dragon's scales are delineated by fine incising. The bluish white glaze is of high quality. The skilled craftsmanship indicates that this piece was probably made at the official Punwŏn kilns.

I

PRUNUS VASE

Inlaid celadon ware; Koryŏ dynasty; 12th/13th century
Ht. 42·1 cm. Diam. 24·5 cm.
Collection of Mr Hyung-pil Chun

This *mae-pyŏng* vase with its elaborate inlaid decoration is one of the largest and finest in existence. Its beauty and grace are enhanced by the skill with which the potters executed their *sanggam*, or inlaying, technique. This unique method of decorating pottery consisted of first cutting out a design in the body of the vessel and then filling the incisions with white or black slip. The excess slip was carefully smoothed away and the vessel was glazed and fired. According to some authorities, a preliminary biscuit firing was given before the glazing.

At the top of the vase, round the small mouth, is a band of *ju-i* sceptre-heads, and at the foot is a band of tall lotus petals. The remainder of the vase is decorated with an overall pattern of forty-six roundels outlined by white outer and black inner rings, inside each of which is a crane flying among clouds. The space between the roundels is occupied by further designs of cranes flying downwards, twenty-three in all, and numerous stylized clouds. The eyes, legs, beaks and head-plumes of the cranes are inlaid in black, while their heads, necks, wings and bodies are inlaid in white, as are the surrounding clouds. The glaze is dark green with profuse crazing.